THOMAS LINACRE c1460-1524
First President of the College 1518-24
Henry Weekes. 1870

GRAVE AND LEARNED MEN: THE PHYSICIANS, 1518–1660

First published in Great Britain in 2017 by Little, Brown

Copyright © Royal College of Physicians and Louella Vaughan 2017

The moral right of the authors has been asserted.

Unless otherwise indicated, all images are from the RCP collections and all photography is by Mike Fear.

Designed by Emil Dacanay and Sian Rance, D.R. ink

A CIP catalogue record for this book is available from the British Library.

ISBN 978-1-4087-0632-9

Printed in China

COVER: John Dee performing an experiment before Queen Elizabeth I, oil painting by Henry Gillard Glindoni (Wellcome Library, London)
PAGE 1: Thomas Linacre
OPPOSITE: An anatomical dissection in an anatomy theatre, c. 1615

500
REFLECTIONS ON THE RCP
1518-2018

GRAVE AND LEARNED MEN: THE PHYSICIANS, 1518–1660

Louella Vaughan

Royal College of Physicians

Inscription around portrait: *Obijt 1573 æt:63.* IOHANNES CAIUS REGIS EDOUARDI VI. REGINÆ ET ELISABETHÆ ANG: MEDICUS

Talis erat CAIUS *medicâ prælustris ab arte,*
Hic qualem facili sculptor in ære dedit.

hh 4.

FOREWORD

The Royal College of Physicians was founded, by Royal Charter, in 1518 by King Henry VIII. Few professional organisations have been in continuous existence for so long, and over its five-hundred-year history the College has been at the centre of many aspects of medical life. Its principal purpose is to promote the highest standards of medical practice in order to improve health and healthcare, and its varied work in the field is held in high regard. Currently, the College has over thirty thousand members and fellows worldwide. Over the years it has also accumulated a distinguished library, extensive archives and a collection of portraits and other treasures, and has been housed in a number of notable buildings. As part of its quincentennial commemoration, a series of ten books has been commissioned. Each book features fifty reflections, thereby making a total of five hundred, intended to be a meditation on, and an exploration of, aspects of the College's work and its collections over its five-hundred-year history.

This volume is the first of a pair that considers the College history. It takes the form of an extended essay, focusing on fifty aspects of the history, and covers the period from 1518 to 1660. Dr Vaughan is a physician and Fellow of the College who has an academic background in the history of medicine, and so is an ideal person to have taken on this task. The book is a fascinating exposition of the early history, warts and all, of the institution and will be of interest to both doctors and historians.

The College's grateful thanks are offered to all who have helped in all stages of production of this book, and especially to Julie Beckwith, Head of the Library at the College, who has worked hard on providing the illustrations for the book and to Sian Rance, the designer who has put the illustrations together to such good effect.

Simon Shorvon –

**Simon Shorvon, Harveian Librarian, Royal College of Physicians
Series Editor**

OPPOSITE: John Caius

CONTENTS

INTRODUCTION

It was a great honour and privilege to be asked to contribute to the '500 Reflections' series celebrating the five-hundredth anniversary of the founding of the Royal College of Physicians.

It was tempting to write a wholly celebratory history of the College, portraying it as a great institution processing inevitably from triumph to triumph. While there is, indeed, much to heap praise upon, the College stands accused by professional historians of a multiplicity of sins, from the unscrupulous grabbing and hoarding of power, to stubborn intellectual backwardness via overweening pride and vanity. For all that these accusations are often driven by post-Marxist, post-Foucauldian views of history and the world, which espy any type of institution with suspicion, if not hostility, the College cannot be entirely absolved. As it was, at its very heart, a licensing and regulatory body, it is inevitable that its history should be littered with spats, disputes and lawsuits. It was also riven by intellectual arguments, fell prey to petty jealousies and frequently had difficulty in containing the personalities of its more domineering members. I have tried, as far as possible, to be even-handed and have refrained on passing judgements. The past is another country – the College did things differently there. But I have attempted to unpack and explain *why* the College and its members did what they did by mapping out the internal politics of and intellectual divisions within the College and linking these to the inexorable march of events and societal changes outside it.

The structure of this pair of books also requires some explanation. This book and the first half of the next book, covering the period from the founding of the College through to the mid-nineteenth century, are meant to be read as a single extended essay. The reasons for this are two-fold. First, while I do not always believe in 'long histories', it remains that within fifty years of its foundation the College found itself trapped by a series of dilemmas. The most important and persistent of these was the fundamental and existential question of what its ultimate purpose was. This was resolved only with the Medical Act and the establishment of the General Medical Council in 1858.

The second reason is that the history of the College has been written before, in a four-volume series. Volumes 3 and 4, which cover the period from the mid-nineteenth century onwards, are excellent; the fourth volume by Asa Briggs being a prime example of what of a social history of an institution should be. The first two volumes on the earlier period, written by Sir George Clark, while exceptionally thorough from an antiquarian perspective, are 'indigestible'. Further, they have been surpassed in terms of scholarship by the historical excavations of Margaret Pelling, Charles Webster and Harold J. Cook.

I have tried to meld the main findings from these key authors, along with a number of insights from my own work on the eighteenth century, into a single, overarching narrative, which should be read alongside, but also as a partial corrective to, the Clark volumes. The story will then be picked up in the next book in this series by Sir Richard Thompson, who gives an overview of the key achievements of the College since the Medical Act, bringing us into the twenty-first century. I have used 'asides' to discuss points of interest that sit outside of the main narrative structure and to pose interesting questions.

The writing of such a 'long history' of an institution brings with it a number of challenges. The attentive reader will notice that more weight is given to the seventeenth and eighteenth centuries than to the sixteenth. This is quite simply because the further one goes back in time, the poorer the primary sources become. Far more is known about relatively minor episodes in the early modern period than it has been possible to recover about the founding of the College. Then there is the fact that most College 'business' was done behind closed doors. This was not the result of deliberate duplicity, but is rather a product of how medical practice was conducted and the highly 'clubbable' nature of male English society at that time. Men who meet and talk most days leave few traces of their conversations. Given that Richard and I had only 40,000 words in which to cover 500 years, there will inevitably be readers who think that important episodes in the College's history have been wrongfully excluded or had insufficient attention paid to them. To these readers, we can only apologise.

It is hoped that these slim volumes will, if nothing else, act as a reminder of what a great act of faith the founding of the College was. It was the embodiment of the Humanist notion that intellectual and moral discipline, coupled with feelings of benevolence, could lead humans out of the darkness and into the light of a harmonious and civilised society. The College was founded for the service of the realm, so that the sickness, decay and suffering that accompanied the lives of all men and women, rich or poor, could be alleviated to the greater benefit of mankind. Thomas Linacre, its first President, spent his last days securing the future of the College and was the first in a long line of physicians who held fast to these great ideals. Through war, rebellion and revolution they fought to ensure the College's survival and to push back the darkness. Some 500 years later and still the light shines on.

THANKS

The seeds for these volumes were first planted during the conference held in honour of the five-hundredth anniversary of Thomas Linacre's attendance at the University of Padua. I remain grateful to Linda Luxon, College Treasurer, for the invitation to attend and to Daniela Marrone and Gaetano Thiene, both of the University of Padua, for organising the event. The conversations that I had with the other historians there, including Daniela, Jonathan Woolfson and Fabio Zampieri, were crucial in shaping the section on the founding of the College. It was also a pleasure at the conference to spend time with my former Cambridge supervisor, Andrew Cunningham, who was as stimulating and thought-provoking as always.

The support given to me by Julie Beckwith and her team, particularly Pamela Forde and Peter Basham, at the library of the Royal College of Physicians was outstanding. I can only hope that I have done a modicum of justice to their knowledge of the archives and collections of the College. I would like to thank William Schupbach, Librarian for the Wellcome Trust's iconographic collections, for his time and for sharing with me his expert knowledge of the pictorial history of the College.

I am particularly grateful to Simon Shorvon for inviting me to author these two volumes and for being tirelessly patient and kind. It is a privilege to have Richard Thompson as co-author and I give him thanks for semi-volunteering for the task and for doing such a sterling job. I would like again to give my apologies to Candace Imison for being periodically distracted from other duties by the past and thank her for her tolerance. Lastly, I would like to dedicate these volumes to Margaret Pelling. Her formidable work on the College greatly informed these volumes and I am, as always, grateful for her fierce intellectual integrity, her academic generosity and her friendship.

A FEW NOTES ON THE TEXT

The term 'Physick' is used to specifically denote medicine as practised according to the principles of Galen.

I have used the spelling of names as they appear in Munk's Roll rather than using modernised versions.

William Harvey demonstrates the circulation of the blood to King Charles I

THE FOUNDING OF THE COLLEGE

London at the time of Henry VIII. From the book *Short History of the English People* by J.R. Green, published London, 1893 (Classic Image/Alamy stock photo)

THE GREAT FOUNDATION STORY

As befits any great institution, the College has its own *aition*, or myth, of its foundation, complete with a hero, villains, an ingenious plan and a triumph so resounding that it is still celebrated centuries later. According to John Freind, the first English historian of the College, the hero of the story is Thomas Linacre. On returning to London after more than a decade abroad, Linacre was alarmed at the state of the English medical profession, which was dominated by 'illiterate Monks and Empiricks'. Heavily influenced by his experiences in Italy, where the medical profession was actively involved in its own organisation and regulation, he conceived of a plan to establish a 'corporate Society of Physicians'. Such a corporate Society would:

> *not only create a good understanding and unanimity amongst his own Profession, which itself was an excellent thought, but to make them more useful to the publick: and he imagin'd that by separating them from the vulgar* Empiricks *and setting upon such a reputable foot of distinction, there wou'd always arise a spirit of emulation among men liberally educated which wou'd animate them in pursuing their inquiries into the* Nature of Diseases *and the* Methods of Cure*, for the benefit of mankind.*

Using his interests at court, Linacre gained the support of the most powerful men in the realm – King Henry VIII and his Lord Chancellor, Cardinal Wolsey – with the King granting his letters patent under the Great Seal incorporating the President and the College or Commonalty of the Faculty of Medicine of London on 23 September 1518. The charter gave the College the power to control the practice of medicine in London and to 'make such Statutes and Ordinances as they, from time to time, shou'd think most expedient for the publick Service'. Thus Linacre and the other College founders vanquished the Empiricks, banished the Monks and enlisted themselves in service to the English realm, 'with regard to their own dignity, the good of the people, and in particular to the honour of the Universities'.[1]

The direct evidence of the College's early history is distressingly slight, but there is little to argue with in terms of the bare facts. Linacre did go to Italy, was influenced by his time there and, on his return, convinced the King to support the establishment of the College. But the casting of characters into storybook roles conceals the true state of affairs immediately prior to the founding of the College. It also fails to capture exactly what it was that Linacre was trying to do, the constellation of factors at play in the founding of the College and the real extent of his success.

In order to better understand these matters, I will turn first to the hero of the piece and his perceived enemies – Thomas Linacre and the motley assortment of medical practitioners of London.

There could be no more
suitable father for the founding
of the College. Educated,
cultivated, sophisticated, he
had ... developed a reputation
as a leading scholar.

THE VIRTUES OF THOMAS LINACRE

Thomas Linacre's early life is lost in the shadows. What is clear is that he was born around 1460, and received his early education at the Canterbury Cathedral School under the direction of William Sellyng before going up to Oxford University in 1480. Shortly after becoming a fellow of All Souls, Linacre was invited by the Italian-educated Sellyng to accompany him on a diplomatic mission to Italy. Linacre went with Sellyng as far as Florence, where he became the pupil of Angelo Poliziano, the highly talented scholar and poet who was tutor to Lorenzo di Medici's sons. Fired with an enthusiasm for Greek scholarship, Linacre immersed himself in the libraries of Florence and Rome, before travelling to Padua, where he commenced his medical studies in 1492. Linacre demonstrated his remarkable intellectual prowess in his final examinations, impressing the medical faculty with excellence and elegance in his *viva voce*. He remained in Italy for another three years, establishing a reputation as 'a man who knows Greek and Latin perfectly well and excels in all disciplines'.[2]

On his return to Oxford in 1499, he became a member of the group of brilliant scholars. Coalesced around Desiderius Erasmus, the group included two friends from his Italian sojourn, William Grocyn and William Latimer, and John Colet. After devoting time to a number of Greek translations, he was called to court as the tutor of Arthur, the Prince of Wales. There he could be seen 'striding amongst the nobles of the royal court, wearing a crimson gown reaching to his ankles, and a full cloak of black velvet thrown

across his shoulders'.[3] It is unclear when he took up medical practice in London, but he was appointed royal physician on the accession of Henry VIII in 1509. He rapidly acquired a small but highly influential clientele, including Cardinal Wolsey, Archbishop William Warham and Bishop Fox.

There could be no more suitable father for the founding of the College. Educated, cultivated, sophisticated, he had dined with the foremost princes of Europe, developed a reputation as a leading scholar in not one but two disciplines and consorted on a daily basis with the most powerful men in the realm. Linacre was a true Renaissance man.

A charlatan with assistants addresses a crowd, 15th century (Wellcome Library, London)

A significant portion of the London marketplace was entirely unregulated and it teemed with a variety of types of practitioner – blood-letters, nurses, midwives, charlatans, quacks and wise-women.

THE BUSTLE OF THE MEDICAL MARKETPLACE

If Linacre's reputation is well deserved, the highly dichotomised depiction of him and his band of university-educated physicians battling to save the populace from 'the endeavours of wicked men…who profess medicine rather because of their own avarice than in any assurance of good conscience' is far from accurate.[4] The medieval medical marketplace was highly complex, with a diverse variety of practitioners peddling their skills, services and wares to the public. It was also surprisingly sophisticated in many aspects, and portions of it were far from unregulated.

The bulk of medical services were provided, in different forms, by the barbers, the surgeons and the apothecaries, all of whom were already regulated through the guild structures that proliferated during the early medieval period. The apothecaries, who compounded and dispensed drugs as well as selling herbs and spices, belonged to the Worshipful Company of Grocers, which could trace its origins back to the founding of the Guild of Pepperers in 1180. The relationship between the barbers and the surgeons was more complex, but their organisations were no less well established. The Guild of Barbers, whose members cut hair, shaved and performed minor surgeries such as the lancing of boils, blood-letting and the extraction of teeth, dated back to 1308. Although the surgeons formed their own unincorporated fellowship in 1368, the Barbers' Guild retained the power to oversee surgical practice, a right retained after it became a company in 1462 by royal charter. These guilds and companies not only oversaw training and regulated standards, but also provided corporate identity to skilled crafts- and tradesmen.

Yet a significant portion of the London marketplace was entirely unregulated and it teemed with a variety of other types of practitioner – blood-letters, nurses, midwives, charlatans, quacks and wise-women. While it may seem reasonable to cast these practitioners as at the very least 'illiterate', if not downright dangerous to the public, it is evident that the public did not view them in this way. Unsurprisingly at a time when virtually all people were familiar with sickness and suffering, matters of health were of great interest to most individuals and they were active seekers after medical information. Moreover, they were usually less interested in cure than they were in prognostication. The search for a degree of certainty about outcomes led the ill person, almost regardless of status or wealth, to consult with 'a whole flock of practitioners and attendants all making entrances and exits as if in a rather frenetic play'.[5]

OVERLEAF: King Henry VIII with the barber surgeons, from the studio of Hans Holbein the younger, inscribed, 1541 (RCSSC/P 106) (© Museums at the Royal College of Surgeons)

An apothecary mixing medicines (Interfoto/Alamy stock photo)

As the universities were also concerned with character, this education marked the physician as a man of great learning, discernment and judgement, allowing potential patients to be assured of his medical knowledge as well as his social and professional deportment.

THE IDENTITY OF THE MEDIEVAL PHYSICIAN

So where did the physicians sit within the medical marketplace and what distinguished them from all other practitioners? The short answer is that the tiny handful of physicians cared for a relatively small section of the upper and wealthier middle classes. They were distinguished from all other practitioners by virtue of a long and elaborate education, which required ten to twelve years of study, ideally at one of the two English universities or on the Continent.

They had to first undertake a bachelor's degree in philosophy. Only after six years of study, the demonstration of a firm grasp of the liberal arts and sciences in university examinations and the award of the Master of Arts could they commence study in the higher faculties, such as medicine, theology and law. The length of the medical degree itself varied between universities and ranged from three to six years. The requirements for an MD were hearing lectures on prescribed books, participation in disputations and success in oral examinations, leaving the physicians with an expert ability to diagnose disease, formulate complex regimes for the restoration of health and predict outcomes. As befitting someone so educated, an Oxbridge medical degree conferred the right to practise throughout England. As the universities were also concerned with character, this education marked the physician as a man of great learning, discernment and judgement, allowing potential patients to be assured of his medical knowledge as well as his social and professional deportment.

Five old apothecaries in an apothecary's shop. An apprentice works with a pestle and mortar in the background (Wellcome Library, London)

In reality, the physicians were not rigidly demarcated from all other types of practitioner. Their training via the universities rather than serving an apprenticeship did separate them from the apothecaries and the barber-surgeons, as well as the rabble, but nor were they an entirely homogenous group. Medical training on the Continent could be undertaken in markedly less time, with the graduate being able to have his degree 'incorporated' at Oxford or Cambridge upon the payment of fees and examination by the medical faculty. Continental degrees themselves also varied. While some were even more rigorous and prescriptive than Oxbridge, others granted degrees upon the student demonstrating the faintest modicum of medical knowledge, again for a fee. Hence the MD was not entirely a badge of quality for either English physicians or the small number of foreign doctors living in London.

Men, in particular clergymen, who had undertaken some medical studies at university without bothering to take or pass the MD or to incorporate foreign degrees blurred these demarcations further. Estimates have suggested that these university-educated 'irregular practitioners' outnumbered their fully fledged medical counterparts.

The professional boundaries that dictated (for the most part) that the physicians diagnosed and prescribed, the apothecaries dispensed and the barber-surgeons incised also made the three professions mutually interdependent. Only occasionally could one type of practitioner provide the patient with all the aspects of care required. Relationships of respect, trust and mutual self-interest were frequent, particularly between the physicians and the apothecaries, with patients being referred between practitioners in both directions.

AN ASIDE ABOUT HUMORAL MEDICINE

Concepts of health and disease at the time of the founding of the College were derived from the writings of the ancient Greeks. For Hippocrates, the 'father' of medicine, wrote of the humours:

> *The Human body contains blood, phlegm, yellow bile and black bile. These are the things that make up its constitution and cause its pains and health. Health is primarily that state in which these constituent substances are in the correct proportion to each other, both in strength and quantity, and are well mixed. Pain occurs when one of the substances presents either a deficiency or an excess...* [6]

Each of the humours was produced by a different organ: black bile by the spleen, yellow bile by the gall bladder, phlegm by the lungs and blood by the liver. They were

OPPOSITE: A surgeon treats a patient

3 Corn du Sart
169.

Four Humors, from *Book of Alchemy* by Thurn-Heisser, Leipzig, Germany, 1574 (Photo Researchers, Inc/Alamy stock photo)

possessed of paired qualities (hot/cold, dry/wet), which corresponded to the four elements of the earth and the four seasons, and they influenced temperament. So, for example, phlegm was cold and wet, corresponded to water and winter, and was associated with the calmer aspects of personality. The production of humours was affected by the external environment by factors such as diet, sleep, exercise and the weather, as well as mental and emotional states.

The cause of disease was highly individualised, with an infinite variety of factors causing sometimes subtle, sometimes overt, imbalances in the humours which then manifested as pain or other bodily dysfunctions. Diagnosis depended on an accounting of the factors possibly at play and cure on the rebalancing of the humours using allopathic herbal remedies, change in the environment or habit, and physical methods of 'draining' the humours, such as blood-letting or purgatives.

Humoral concepts encouraged patients, potential and otherwise, to become health-literate, as the monitoring of health and the making of adjustments to their diet, lifestyles and environment offered the opportunity to stave off disease. What a physician could offer to the layman included three main things: the knowledge and experience to make subtle diagnoses, the ability to prognosticate, and the prescription of sophisticated regimes, including compounded drugs. For this type of knowledge, the physician had to have a deep understanding of the works of Galen.

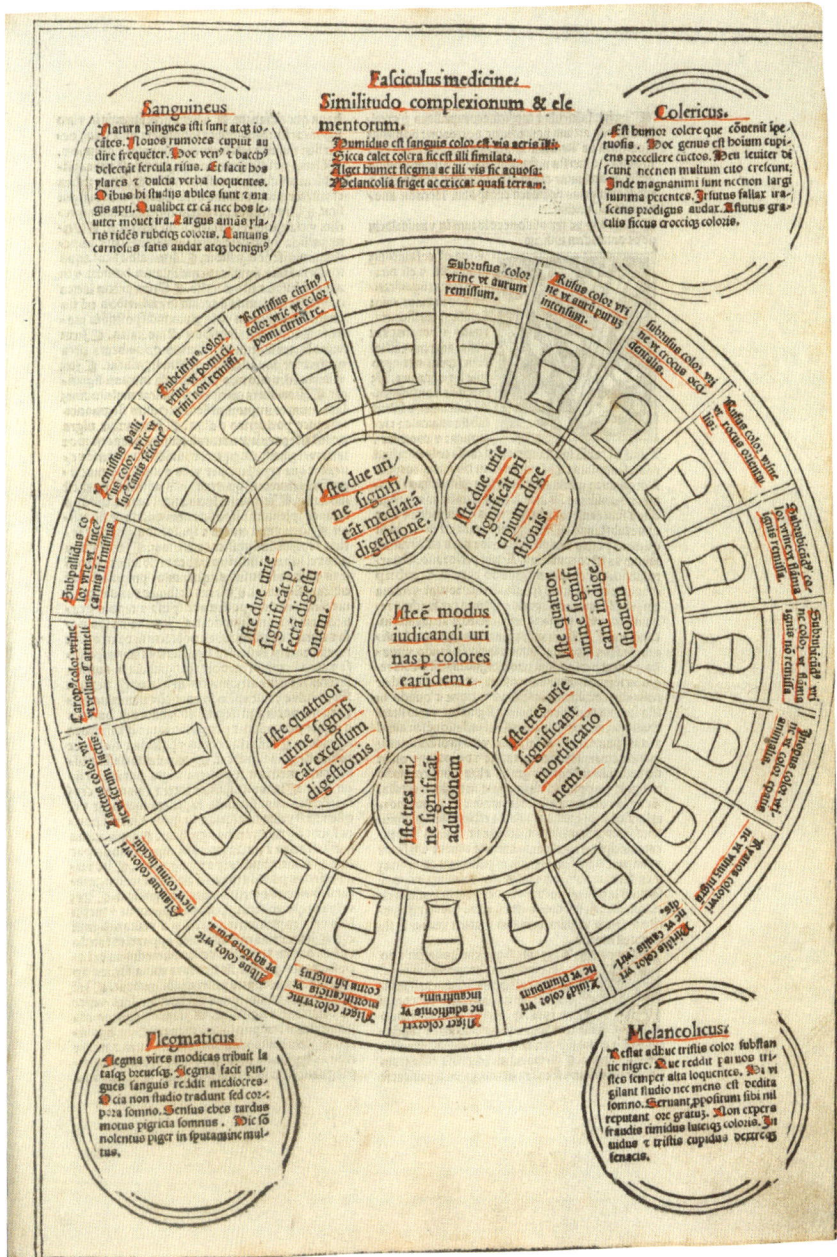

Urine wheel in *Fasciculus medicinae* by Johannes de Ketham, printed in Venice, 1500. Urine was thought to reveal imbalances of the four humours. At the edge of the wheel are 20 descriptions of the colour and characteristics of the urine samples. Inside this are representations of urine flasks. The flasks fall into seven categories according to what they indicate about the patient's health. The central roundel gives the 'method of diagnosing by the colours of urines'

Galien natif de Pergame ville d'Asie, excellent Medecin viuoit du temps des Empereurs Antonin le Philosophe et de Commodus, on tient qu'il a vescu 140 ans.

Galen

THE MEDICAL POPE OF THE MIDDLE AGES

While Hippocrates may have been the 'father' of Greek medicine, the development of medieval medicine in the West rested almost entirely on the works of Galen. Aelius Galenus was born in Pergamon (modern Turkey) in AD 129. Left independently wealthy by his architect father, he travelled extensively in pursuit of a medical education. Eventually settling in Rome and despite his pugnacious temperament, he developed a reputation as one of the finest physicians and scholars of the age.

In common with most of his medical contemporaries, Galen saw himself as a philosopher as well as a physician. However, he did not accept the clear distinctions between the medical empiricists, who argued that medical progress was possible only through direct experimentation, and the rationalists, who valued theoretical hypotheses. Instead, he espoused an approach that fused both the empirical and rational through a combination of theory, observation and direct experimentation. Through the application of this approach to the study of anatomy, he made key insights into the circulatory, nervous and respiratory systems.

Galen's restless energies resulted in an astonishing outpouring of medical works, with his surviving books making up fully half of the extant literature of ancient Greece. It is not surprising, then,

Hippocrates

that his books were among the first to make their way from Constantinople to Europe in the eleventh century, where they were rapidly incorporated into the curricula of the early Italian universities.

While the sheer obscurity of some of Galen's works and the poor translations from Greek into Latin and Arabic posed substantial problems to medieval medical scholars, the breadth and comprehensiveness of Galen's works provided a logical course of study to be presented to medical students, covering physiology, hygiene, aetiology of disease, semiotics of disease, and therapeutics. This rapidly solidified into a defined corpus of medical knowledge that was eventually taught throughout the whole of the West. While other authors were included in the medical curriculum, the simple fact is that it was not possible to become a physician without being entirely intimate with the works and philosophy of Galen.

FIRST ATTEMPTS AT REGULATION

The practice of Physick in England was highly unusual in not being self-regulated, the process of incorporation of vocational groups having been a key feature of urban development in the medieval period. The lack of a charter denied the physicians specific rights, privileges and commercial advantages, as well as an 'immortal collective personality which provided the key to enhanced social status'.[7]

There had been two failed attempts to regulate medicine in the previous century. In 1421, the 'Physicians Petition' asked Parliament to control English Physick through the universities. The English sheriffs should assemble every medical practitioner in England at either Oxford or Cambridge, where they would be put to a 'trewe and streyte examinacion'.[8] Thereafter, anyone who continued to practise without a licence would be liable for a fine or imprisonment. Surprisingly, given the logistical requirements of such a venture, the petition was met with a favourable answer. Further meetings took place, but nothing seems to have come of it.

The efforts of Gilbert Kymer, a priest and later chancellor of the University of Oxford, were more successful in 1423, when he and a group of like-minded men presented a petition to the mayor and aldermen of London to establish a guild or 'Comminalte' of physicians and surgeons. The Comminalte was to be organised along the lines of the Inns of Court, with the purpose of educating and regulating all types of medical practitioner, as well as providing treatment for the poor. The petition was granted and it presided over a single hearing before collapsing in the face of resistance from the Barbers' Company and a falling-out between its two main patrons.

PHYSICK AND THE ECCLESIASTICAL COURTS

The founding story of the College strongly suggests that Linacre was prompted into action immediately upon his return from Italy, having found Physick regulated by the 'illiterate Monks' of the ecclesiastical courts. A closer reading of the dates suggests a rather different course of events. Linacre had, in fact, been home for several years before the ecclesiastical courts were granted the powers to regulate Physick and Surgery in 1511. The act in question argued that this was necessary:

Foreasmuch as the Science and Cunning of Physick and Surgery (to the perfect knowledge whereof be requisite both great Learning and ripe Experience) is daily within this realm exercised by ignorant persons…in which they partly use Sorcery and Witchcraft, partly apply such Medicines unto the Disease as be noious, and nothing meet therefore, to the high

Displeasure of God, great infamy to the Faculty and the grievous Hurt, Damage, and Destruction of many of the King's liege People, most especially of them that cannot discern the cunning from the uncunning.[9]

The act stipulated that no person within the City of London, nor within seven miles of it, should 'exercise and occupy' as a physician or surgeon except where he were first examined, appointed and admitted by the Bishop of London (Robert Fitz-James) or the Dean of St Paul's (John Colet). Outside the City precinct, no one was to practise as a physician or surgeon unless they had undergone a similar process of approval by the local bishop or his vicar general. Anyone who practised without first being found fit would be fined £5 per month until they ceased practice or submitted to examination. The system would rely on informants, incentivised by the promise of half the fines. The universities were to retain their traditional rights to grant licences to practise through the realm, although this was no longer exclusive.

In many ways, the act was an extension of the powers already held by the Church. In London, the Bishop and the Dean had granted licences to surgeons since their guild was founded. The Church also had a sophisticated administration system in place, capable of carrying through with the proposal, at least in bigger centres. The surgeons, given that they were already partly under ecclesiastical control, rapidly fell in line with the examination and admission of seventy-two surgeons in 1514. Yet, once again, the scheme seems to have fallen apart after the initial burst of enthusiasm, with surgeons no longer bothering to take out licences after a year or two. There is no mention of any physicians being examined, although this may reflect a gap in the historical records. This collapse may be a reflection of the increasing schism between the conservative Fitz-James and the more radical Colet over the latter's desires for Church reform.

Anyone who practised without first being found fit would be fined £5 per month until they ceased practice or submitted to examination.

John Colet (© The Chapter of St Paul's Cathedral)

So, not only did the Church fail to gain effective control over the medical profession, but the characterisation of men such as Fitz-James and Colet as 'illiterate Monks' is not just harsh, but patently untrue. They were both highly talented and able men, with Colet considered a great classical scholar. Moreover, the Church in England was at the very height of its powers, with the bishops also occupying key roles in secular government.

THE COLLEGE CHARTER OF 1518

Having explored the background of the founding of the College in more detail, perhaps having revealed that heroic physicians were not so distant from other medical practitioners and that the attempt to regulate medicine was not entirely novel, we turn to the central act, the granting of the Charter of Incorporation to the President and College.

The proposal for the formation of the College appears to have been put to Henry VIII and Wolsey in 1517, with the King granting the charter on 23 September 1518. The charter, particularly in comparison with the later College statutes, was a straightforward document. It commenced with an iteration of the concerns regarding the unregulated state of medicine:

> *We have chiefly and before all things necessary to withstand in good time the audacity of those wicked men who shall profess medicine more for the sake of their own avarice than from the assurance of any good conscience, whereby very many inconveniences may ensure to the rude and credulous populace.*[10]

It acknowledges the petition of 'the grave men' – the three royal physicians, John Chambre, Thomas Linacre and Fernandez de Victoria; three other physicians, Nicholas Halsewell, Giovanni Franceschi and Robert Yaxley; and the Lord Chancellor, Cardinal Wolsey – as well as the desire to imitate 'the example of other well governed cities in Italy and many other nations'. It then commands:

> *to be instituted a perpetual College of learned and grave men who shall publicly exercise medicine in our City of London and the suburbs, and within seven miles from that City on every side: Whose care it will be, as we hope, both for their own honour and in the name of the public benefit, as well as to discourage the unskilfulness and temerity of the knavish men whom we have mentioned, by their own example and gravity, as to punish the same by our laws lately enacted…*

In addition to restricting the practice of medicine to those who had been admitted to the College, its regulatory powers extended to 'foreign physicians whomsoever

Charter and seal of the College of Physicians, 1518

in any manner frequenting…the same City', as well as to the apothecaries, through the granting of 'the oversight and scrutiny of all manner of medicines'. Failure to comply with the College regulations meant punishment by 'fines, amendments and imprisonment of their bodies, and by other reasonable and fitting means'. To these ends, the petitioners and their colleagues in London were established as *unum corpus et communitas perpetua sive Collegium perpetuum*', one body and perpetual commonalty or College, with the rights to perpetual succession, a common seal and to the possession of lands to the value of £12.

The charter contained a number of instructions regarding the conduct of the College. The President and College members were granted the ability to make 'lawful and honest assemblies of themselves, and statutes, and ordinances for the wholesome government… of the College'. Annual elections were to be held for the role of President, who was to 'oversee, superintend and govern for that year the College'. Four Censors would also be elected to 'have the oversight and scrutiny, correction and government of all and singular physicians' in London. Members having committed or having been tried for unlawful acts were to be expelled from the College. Finally, the charter also exempted physicians from service on all assizes, juries and inquests in London and elsewhere.

WRESTING POWER FROM VESTED INTERESTS

Three organisations already had claims to the powers newly vested in the College – the universities of Oxford and Cambridge, the Church and the vocational guilds. A university MD conferred the right to practise medicine throughout England, while the Church had the right to examine and license physicians and surgeons to practise in London. The guilds controlled the apothecaries, the trade in drugs and spices, and the barbers.

The College's charter, then, was a direct challenge to the authority of all these august bodies. This challenge is even more remarkable when one considers that at this time all power flowed from one of only two sources – the King or the Church. In the case of the ecclesiastical courts, the relationships with the fonts of power were clear and direct. The universities, less overtly, effectively embodied the power of the *regnum* or the *sacertdotium*, having been confirmed in its status and granted specific rights and privileges by its founding authority, such as the Pope or the monarch. This, in turn, allowed them to protect and perpetuate learning and scholarship, to the greater glory of the realm. A similar relationship existed between the guilds and the *regnum*, which were also granted rights and privileges by the King.

NEITHER FISH NOR FOWL?

Superficially, the College borrowed from aspects of all three of the medical licensing bodies. It claimed no new powers that had not been granted in any of the earlier attempts to regulate medical practice or to the Oxbridge universities and, indeed, the College's right to license was identical to those previously granted to the Bishop of London. It was explicitly modelled on the Italian medical guilds and had a passing resemblance to the City companies that governed other aspects of London mercantile life.

It has been argued that by making the College an amalgamation of other licensing organisations, it could usurp and consolidate their collective powers into single body, superior and more effective than any of the original three. While it is undoubtedly true that the founders were keen to shore up the authority of the infant College, there were subtle differences that signalled that the College was not just a conglomerate of the useful bits of other entities.

In the first instance, the highly hierarchical structure of the London guilds and the ecclesiastical courts was entirely absent. The charter mentioned only two types of office bearer, the President and the four Censors, the role of the latter being more about external regulation than the smooth running of the College. There was no attempt to differentiate between other members of the College with regard to the participation in its business or election of President. Indeed, the desire of equality of members was reflected in the use of the word *socius*, which translates as 'companion, partner or colleague' and was commonly used in the late medieval period to denote 'he that keeps company with another'.[11]

The guilds had clear criteria for membership. While it was possible to join a guild following an examination and the payment of a fee, the usual route was via a highly structured apprenticeship. In contrast, the charter actually failed to include any mention of what sort of skills or knowledge were required in order to join the College – it simply enjoined that 'physicians' had to be admitted to the College in order to practise medicine in London. The use of the word 'physician' does, however, imply someone in possession of an MD from a university, and the use of the word 'College' directly links the new organisation with Oxford and Cambridge. Yet the charter contains no mention of education or teaching, key university and guild functions.

THE LONG SHADOW OF PADUA

So what *was* the purpose of the College, if not to simply take over medical regulation in England? We can begin to find the answer to this by looking to the University of Padua, where Linacre and John Chambre had both studied medicine.

England had found itself, by reasons of war and cultural insularity, cut off from the first flowerings of the Italian Renaissance. But by the late 1400s, the promise held out by the Humanist movement that the richness of the ancient texts

There were subtle differences that signalled that the College was not just a conglomerate of the useful bits of other entities.

John Chambre, one of the founding fellows of the College of Physicians. Chambre was first in order of the six physicians mentioned in the letters patent of Henry VIII for the foundation of the College

Thomas More

The leading university for the study of civic Humanism was the University of Padua, which was also the home of the most advanced medical school in Europe.

not only offered more perfect forms of knowledge, but also a way of bringing to fruition a better and more civilised society, was beginning to capture the imaginations of the English ruling and intellectual elites. The Humanists saw the depictions of ancient Greece and Rome as offering visions for the revival of society, an alternative to the perceived barbarism of the Middle Ages. The key to this civic rejuvenation was the fostering of the individual. The classics provided the model of a method, through the study of philosophy, rhetoric and history, that would equip men with the moral and political foundations of good counsel and right judgement in private and public life. Through the Humanist ideals of enlightened rule and diligent scholarship, the perfect civilisation, the 'place of felicity' of Thomas More's *Utopia*, could be created.

The leading university for the study of civic Humanism was the University of Padua, which was also the home of the most advanced medical school in Europe. Following the broader precepts of Humanist studies, the 'medical humanism' taught there was primarily an attempt to reconstruct the original words of the ancient Greek medical sources, particularly Hippocrates and Galen, as the first step towards a reformed

practice of medicine. Moreover, the physician was also to be a philosopher, able to deploy the Greek virtues of reason, wisdom and prudence as well as drawing on his experience to form a 'right judgement' in medical matters. The physician should not only be able to save lives, but to contribute to the cumulative progress of knowledge.

The highly active nature of Humanism was reflected in the administration of the university, which was a form of *Utopia* in itself. While other European universities were highly monastic in nature, Padua was ultimately run by the Venetian Senate, which prioritised profit over virtually all other considerations. This made it a place of extraordinary academic freedom, as teachers sought to attract international fee-paying students with a combination of intellectual rigour and scholastic iconoclasm. Moreover, Padua was virtually devoid of a clerical hierarchy and effectively student-controlled, with a complex system of voting that shaped most aspects of institutional life. This system of voting demanded that students enrolling at the university *live* the teachings that it espoused – the study of philosophy and the participation in public life of the university were part of the same grand thing.

A view of Padua in the 16th century (Prisma Archivo/Alamy stock photo)

THE EXAMPLE OF THE ITALIAN MEDICAL GUILDS

The University of Padua was not the only novel form of institution to which Linacre and Chambre were exposed while on their travels abroad. The charter is clear that imitating the 'well governed cities of Italy' was a highly desirable aspect of the College's foundation. So what did the Italian guilds do that was so different from organisations regulating medical practice in London?

While Italian university towns usually had colleges that were directly linked to the university and the medical faculty, other towns had colleges that were chartered corporations of the local physicians, independent of other bodies. They recruited medical graduates from elsewhere, but were responsible for the control of the practice of medicine in their locality. Along with extensive powers of regulation, their responsibilities extended beyond those usually attached to the English universities or guilds to other aspects of medicine, such as public health, hospital organisation and relief of the sick poor. As such, the Italian medical guilds reflected aspects of civic Humanism – they required the active participation of their members in the public life of their home town.

A NEW TYPE OF ORGANISATION

In view of Linacre and Chambre's experiences in Italy, it becomes clearer that the Charter was not simply proposing an amalgamation of the three organisations already involved in the regulation of medical practice in London. It was proposing a new type of organisation previously unseen in England – a corporation of educated and professional men dedicated not just to overseeing their own affairs, but to an enlightened practice of medicine that extended beyond the usual doctor–patient relationship, in best Humanist fashion, to 'the public benefit'. Moreover, it would be run along Humanist lines, with men working together as equals and colleagues to achieve common goals. The goal, then, of the founders was to build a new type of organisation that would embody and promote by example the very best of all aspects of enlightened medical practice.

Yet the trespassing of the College onto the territory of the Church, the universities and the guilds and its radical nature would so incense all these great and august institutions that it would be not just decades, but centuries, before the sin of the College's usurpation of their powers could be forgiven and forgotten.

THE QUESTION OF TIMING

There remains the key issue of the timing of the founding of the College. If it was, in fact, evident on Linacre's return from Italy that England was suffering from a want of effective medical regulation, then why wait for over a decade before proposing an alternative? Moreover, why didn't he and his fellow physicians more actively oppose the act proposed by Fitz-James and Colet in 1511? Or wait so long after the obvious failure of the ecclesiastical courts to impose effective discipline?

The historical record is not forthcoming with answers to these particular questions. However, it is clear that there was a particular constellation of factors at play in 1517–18 that directly influenced the founding of the College and the particular shape that it took.

PLAGUE AND PESTILENCE

The clearest prompt was the outbreak of plague in 1517. Desperate to curb the epidemic, Cardinal Wolsey directly intervened in matters with a royal proclamation that ordered the marking of doors of infected households and restricting the movements of their inhabitants. While Linacre's initial response was to translate Galenic texts relevant to epidemics, the advantage was seized to propose a medical organisation more capable of intervening in matters of public health than a cardinal.

THE RENAISSANCE PRINCE

The outbreak of plague in 1517 coincided with a precise point in the early reign of Henry VIII. Henry, being a second son, had not been intended for the throne and expressed little interest in matters of statescraft for the first years following his accession in 1509 beyond neutralising a number of key opponents. However, his first forays in war and an increasingly complex and delicate political ballet between the European powers fired Henry's ambition, and he turned to the task of cultivating the greatest Renaissance court in Europe.

Humanism was to be central to Henry's task. Not only had he been the recipient of an outstanding Humanist education at the hands of some of the finest scholars in Europe, but it provided him with a coherent narrative for establishing a great and civilised nation. At the heart of this was the concept of the sovereign ruler – the King was at the centre of the realm and it was his sovereign right to exercise his will. His obligation, however,

Plague doctor

was not to act according to his whims, but to rule for the benefit of his people and to the greater glory of God. For the Renaissance ruler or prince, the task was to become the very embodiment of virtue, to exercise good counsel in all things and act only according to the common good of the realm. The monarch was the arbiter between order and chaos, and the realm prospered when policies that were advantageous, truthful and honourable were advanced.

Humanism, as we have seen, is a philosophy that demands action as well as scholarship. Not only did Henry make his court into a place of great sophistication and creative innovation, he also threw his support behind other organisations that either furthered the Humanist programme, such as St Paul's School, founded by Colet in 1509, or strengthened aspects of civil life, such as new corporations and guilds. The College, with its aspirations to be the very model of all things good and enlightened about Humanist medical practice, clearly elided with Henry's goal of making England the greatest realm in Europe.

Henry VIII

PERSONALITY AND PROFESSIONAL RIVALRIES

Part of the hesitation in the founding of the College can be found in the person of Linacre himself. A man of scholarship rather than action, he was famed for his reluctance even to commit himself to print. So professional rivalry might have played a role in the founding of the College. Linacre and Colet, the Dean of St Paul's, had become well acquainted on Linacre's return to Oxford. When Colet founded St Paul's School in 1509, an elementary Latin grammar was required and Linacre submitted the work *Progymnasmata*. The grounds on which Colet rejected the work

The King was at the centre of the realm and it was his sovereign right to exercise his will. His obligation, however, was not to act according to his whims, but to rule for the benefit of his people and to the greater glory of God.

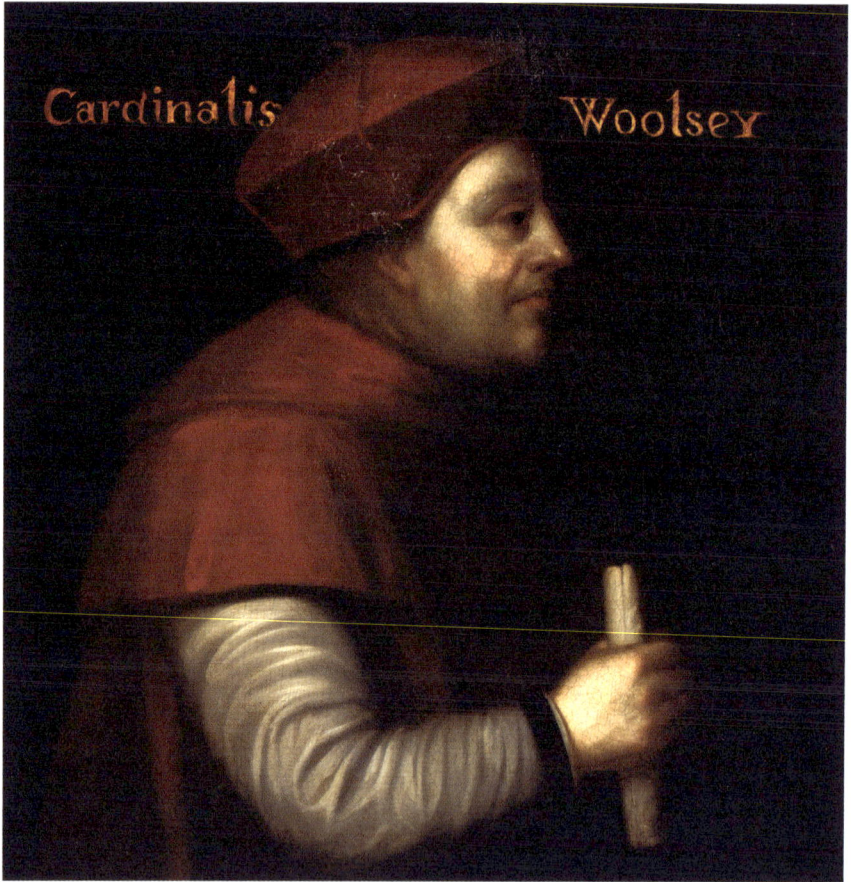

Cardinal Thomas Wolsey

are unclear, but there are lingering hints of sloppy work and even plagiarism. This, followed by Colet's direct incursion on medical territory with his seizure of medical licensing in London, perhaps explains the frostiness between Linacre and Colet that persisted for some years, although they were reconciled by the time of Colet's death in 1519. The episode hints at the possibility of Linacre settling a score in the founding of the College.

The appearance of Wolsey as a petitioner on behalf of the College is also quite remarkable. This has been interpreted as a mark of the perceived importance of the College in helping to contain the outbreak of plague. But Wolsey was never a man to put a good crisis to waste, and the founding of the College likely provided opportunities to cock a snook at his more conservative ecclesiastical opponents, Fitz-James among them, while finding favour with the King.

THE ANATOMY OF AN ANXIOUS ORGANISATION

THE EARLY YEARS

There is no contemporary record of the first years of the College. By 1524, however, regular meetings were being held at the Stone House, Linacre's London house on Knightrider Street. Linacre's will indicates that a 'parlour adioyning to the street'[12] was used for meetings, with an upper room being used for the library.

The first item of business appears to have been the drawing up of the College statutes and the obtaining of an act of Parliament to confirm the charter. But there is little evidence of much other activity – only six more members joined the original six by 1522 and there were only thirty-one members in the period to 1553. The first case against unlicensed medical practitioners was not brought until 1527. The eagerly awaited plans to combat plague never materialised.

In some ways, this inactivity is scarcely surprising as for its first few years the College consisted of only six men, all of whom were busy. Most had demanding patients, while Linacre and Chambre had both taken holy orders and were increasingly preoccupied with other matters. Chambre had been appointed warden of Merton College, while Linacre's declining health spurred him into a flurry of activity that secured his lasting legacy, publishing books and arranging an array of bequests. But it also speaks of a degree of insecurity that was to continue to dog the College during its early history and markedly shape its future.

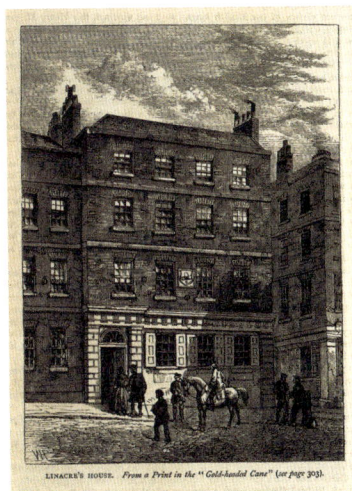

LINACRE'S HOUSE. *From a Print in the " Gold-headed Cane" (see page 303).*

Thomas Linacre's house in Knightrider Street (Wellcome Library, London)

THE ACT AND THE STATUTES

The granting of the charter was not an end to the paperwork required to have a functioning regulatory organisation. There were negotiations to be had with the City of London, an act of Parliament to obtain and statutes governing the more quotidian aspects of the College to be written. While one might expect that the act and the statutes might accurately reflect what was contained in the charter, there were marked differences between the three sets of legal documents and these differences were to be pivotal as to the purpose and function of the College. More importantly, the differences were to become the chief source of contention and dissent within the College, fuelling internal conflicts that often spilt over into the public arena and threatened to tear the College apart.

The act of 1523 was distinct from the charter in a number of ways. Firstly, the act extended the College's powers of regulation from the City of London to encompass 'the exercise or practice in physic through England'. Secondly, it radically reorganised the internal structure of the College. The President was no longer to be chosen from amongst the body of fellows. Rather, the six founding members should form an elite group of 'Elects', who would choose two more members from the commonalty to form a group of eight. This octet would then annually choose the President from among themselves. The position of Elect was to be for life, with surviving Elects choosing a replacement upon the death of one of their number. The simple stipulation in the charter that members of the College should be 'physicians' was replaced with two conditions: members must be 'a Graduate of Oxford or Cambridge' and should be 'profound, sad, and discreet, groundedly learned and deeply studied in physic'.[13] Admission to the College would occur only after examination by the President and three of the eight Elects.

What survives of the earliest statutes is a compendium edited and completed by John Caius in 1563. As noted by Sir George Clark in *A History of the Royal College of Physicians*, although the compendium purports to contain a record of each of the six sets of statutes passed between its founding and 1563, Caius appears to have heavily amended and editorialised these. This makes it impossible to discern what portions of the earlier statutes are recorded as originally passed. What is clear, however, is the state of the statutes in 1563.

In the forty years since its founding, the College had shifted even further from its original charter. It had sought to extend its powers beyond its original mission to license medical practitioners and inspect apothecaries. It saw itself as having the right to 'examine, correct and govern…to learn what were there methods of treatment, to judge medicines'.[14] The College hierarchy was expanded to include: two Consiliarii, who were to settle disputes between the fellows; a pro-President, to take the President's place on his absence; four Censors, who were to identify and judge all practitioners of medicine; and a Beadle, who was to be the chief

Statutes of the College of Physicians, c. 1647

The statutes of 1563 defined what were to be the dominant activities and ideological positions of the College over the next centuries.

College servant. It was swollen again later with the creation of the posts of Registrar, who was to be the keeper of the College records, and Treasurer. All College officers were to be Englishmen and to be chosen by the Elects. Examinations for membership for the College were to be held in four parts, with clear stipulations as to the importance of a knowledge of Galen.

The rules for the governance of the College also became increasingly complex, with multiple rules that choreographed the governance and meetings of the College, making them formal and heavily ceremonial. There were rules outlining the standards for professional conduct for physicians, particularly their relationships with each other and with apothecaries. There was a further restriction on membership, in that clerics and priests could not join the College. The statutes also contained draconian threats to those who did not obey the President or broke their College oaths.

The statutes of 1563 defined what were to be the dominant activities and ideological positions of the College over the next centuries. Its main concern was to regulate medical practitioners, through the mechanism of examination for those who came willingly to the College and through the energetic pursuit of those who did not. Ideologically, it saw itself as a body of learned men, with learning being defined as a Humanist approach to the study of Galen, with a distinct caste system based around education and seniority. As befitting a sober and learned organisation, it was to conduct itself in an appropriately formal manner.

These positions, however, opened up a distance with the charter, which is thrown into sharp relief when it is considered that most of the original founders would have been excluded from either membership or office of the later College. Chambre and Linacre had degrees from Padua, rather than Oxbridge, and along with Halsewell took holy orders; de Victoria and Franceschi were not English. Only Yaxley would have been a suitable candidate for full participation in the business of the College.

More importantly, the fact that the College had seen fit to introduce statutes that usurped the original charter was to become intensely problematic. Both internal and external critics of the College would repeatedly argue that the violation of the charter called into question the whole legitimacy of the College. It would leave it open to charges of being monopolistic and power hungry, of over-reaching its powers and descending into corruption.

AN ASIDE ABOUT COLLEGE CEREMONY

There are no records of the first meetings of the College but, given that they were meetings among equal men in a private house, it might be assumed that they were relatively informal affairs. In contrast, the later statutes are remarkable for the ceremonial

Procession of the President and officers, 2014 (© Hufton + Crow)

intricacies they describe. On College occasions, the members of the College were to process in order of rank, with the President to be preceded by the Beadle, who was to carry the silver caduceus given to the College as a mark of Presidential office. Due deference was to be shown to each rank of College officer, with the President to be addressed as 'Your Excellency'. Only fellows of the College could be seated at the College table, while the lower ranks of the candidates and licentiates (see below) had to remain standing. The College even had a prescribed dress code – 'sober' attire in dark robes without any undue adornments.

Silver caduceus, c.1556, with four serpents and the RCP arms

The members of the College were to process in order of rank, with the President to be preceded by the Beadle, who was to carry the silver caduceus.

John Caius

Not only did he collate the existing statutes in his own hand, he proceeded to make multiple rounds of further changes over the twenty-two years of his sporadic presidency.

THE ANXIETIES OF JOHN CAIUS

The chief architect of the 1563 statutes was John Caius. Born in Norwich, he studied divinity at Gonville Hall, Cambridge, before travelling to Padua to undertake a medical degree. At Padua, he shared a house with the great anatomist Andreas Vesalius and became equally skilled at anatomy as at philology and Humanist philosophy. He joined the College in 1547, without having incorporated his degree in England, and rapidly rose through the ranks, becoming an Elect in 1550 and President for the first of many times in 1555.

Caius took little time in stamping his authority on the College. Despite his outward appearance, being short and having a thin and reedy voice, he was known for being argumentative, bloody-minded with a fuss-budget's attention to minutiae. Accordingly, he proceeded to demonstrate something of an obsession with the College statutes. Not only did he collate the existing statutes in his own hand, he proceeded to make multiple rounds of further changes over the twenty-two years of his sporadic presidency, all seeking to either strengthen the College's licensing powers or to add layers of prescription to the conduct of the College business.

Yet, Caius's obsession was not just a function of his personality. It stemmed from very real anxieties from two sources. Firstly, the role of the College and its authority in a complex medical marketplace where physicians were in the minority and the attempts of the College to impose order had aroused the ire of the apothecaries, the barber-surgeons and the City of London alike. It also reflected the deeper fears that were now stalking most Englishmen. The College had been founded in a period of relative stability in England, with Henry VIII at the peak of his political and intellectual powers. Yet within a few years of the parliamentary act, the realm had been plunged into religious and political turmoil, with Henry divorcing Catherine of Aragon and then splitting from Rome. The College's other main patron, Cardinal Wolsey, was arrested for treason, dying in 1530 before he could be tried. Henry's capriciousness and the zealotry of the Reformation meant that men and institutions alike could never count themselves entirely safe from persecution, no matter how much they may have found his favour. The instability had only worsened after Henry's death, with the boy King Edward VI's reign being marked by economic instability, riots and rebellion. Caius became President only two years after Mary I had deposed Lady Jane Grey and begun, by means of force, to restore Roman Catholicism.

If authority and power flowed from the Crown and the Church and both of these are in turmoil, where then does security rest? For Caius the answer was not in trusting a loosely worded charter, it was in clear definitions and tight regulations. It is no coincidence that the new statutes were virtually identical in design to those used by the Italian guilds.

Caius, in his construction of highly elaborate ceremonies, was also clearly creating visual references to religious ceremonies. By analogy, it has been suggested, Caius was seeking to signify that the College fellows were like the bishops of the Church. Where the bishops had the supreme right to ensure order among the clergy to preserve the spiritual health of the realm, so the 'medical bishops' of the College should exercise their authority over all other medical practitioners to preserve the physical health of England's citizens. To extend the clerical metaphor, it was proposed in 1600 that junior members of the College should present themselves to the College four times per year to 'confess' by giving an account of their past attendances at College meetings and their intentions for the future. The motion was not carried.

It has been argued that Caius was highly motivated by his near hero-worship of Linacre and his desire to secure his legacy. There is likely a degree of truth in this and certainly Caius did what he could to canonise Linacre as the College's patron saint. Yet Caius's obsessive desire to shore up legitimacy extended to similar bouts of obsessiveness with the statutes of the University of Cambridge and the college he was later to refound (Gonville and Caius College). For these, he constructed complex pseudo-traditions and was 'creative' with written records that made claims to antique origins. When engaged in a bitter dispute over which university was not the oldest in just England, but the world, he claimed to have found documents that traced Cambridge's founding back to an exiled Spaniard called Cantaber, in 3588 BC. This raises the possibility that Caius's enthusiasm for Linacre, and the statutes, were yet more attempts to create an illustrious organisational ancestry. Who could question the learning and virtue of an organisation founded by the greatest of all Humanist scholars?

Gonville and Caius College, Cambridge (David Loggan, 1634–92)

THE STATUS OF THE PHYSICIAN

While a number of Caius's concerns and preoccupations were directed by the quirks of his personality and the political upheavals of the time, they also reflect the broader problem of the status of the doctor in English society. Having come very late to the civic party of guilds and corporations, the College had no assured place in the established hierarchy of estates and orders of medieval urban life. The long training required to become a physician also markedly delayed marriage, the establishment of family and the making of a place within the community. This separation from other men of similarly 'middling' status was further marked by the need to emulate the qualities and values of the elite patients to whom they attended. The distance of the physicians from the standard safety nets of other middling sorts, the family, the small business that a son could carry on and a place within a brotherhood of fellow craftsmen made them particularly prone to the vicissitudes of a profession that depended on personal effort and the retention of the favour of patients. The annals of the College are full of the names of men who came to London, tried to make a living and then simply disappeared.

Title page of the annals of the College of Physicians, vol I, 1518–72

The annals of the College are full of the names of men who came to London, tried to make a living and then simply disappeared.

The personification of medicine. A physician stands on a dais. He wears academic dress and his gown is composed of some of the ancient and medieval books which the learned physicians would have read. Elevated by his learning, which ranges across several subjects, the physician stands over two subordinate figures. On the left is an apothecary and on the right is a surgeon (Wellcome Library, London)

EXISTENTIAL DILEMMAS

The purpose, then, of Caius's reshaping of the College and its statutes was to put the legitimacy of the College beyond question in troubled times and ease the collective anxieties of its members about their status and place in the world. However, such existential worries could not be so easily soothed and instead ran in undercurrents through all the activities of the College, bubbling up from time to time into discussions and then dissent around three key issues.

The first was the nagging issue of the true purpose of the College. As a hodge-podge of bits of other organisations – part guild, part university, with a few references to the clergy – and a vague mandate that it ought to be of 'public benefit', this was never entirely clear. Its dominant traceable activity was as a licensing body, but it did not pursue this consistently, opening up the question of whether it should be behaving more like the Humanist organisation it was founded as and promote an intellectual programme. Or should it be intervening in matters of public health?

The second was around the issue of what constituted 'learned medicine'. Even by the time that Caius was enshrining Galen in the statutes, the authority of the ancient Greeks was beginning to be questioned with regard to medical practice. The third lay around the problem of who was a suitable person to be a member of the College. While the College was conceived as a proto-egalitarian organisation, the restrictions on membership in terms of nationality, education and other forms of affiliation were increasingly chafed against.

Given that these issues were to haunt the College from the time of Caius through to the mid-nineteenth century, they are worth laying out in some detail.

THE COLLEGE AS A LICENSING BODY

If activity reflects belief, then the College saw itself first and foremost as a licensing body. It began to exert its rights to police all medical activity shortly after the parliamentary act of 1523 and did so with enthusiasm most of the time. However, its insistence on its right to regulate brought it into regular conflict with three main groups – the apothecaries, the barber-surgeons and the irregular practitioners.

The apothecaries, in particular, found the yoke of the College especially difficult to bear. Although not university trained, the apothecaries were still required to have a firm grasp of the tenets of Galenic medicine and a thorough knowledge of the *materia medica*, the substances used for healing. This made the stipulated boundary between the provision of medical advice, which was the preserve of physicians, and the provision of medical substances, difficult not to cross. It also, coupled with their high civic status, their membership of an ancient and highly respectable guild and their relative wealth, led to a strong sense of apothecaries being as good as the physicians. The College's right to inspect their premises and then to burn drugs and other medicaments when found unsuitable directly attacked the sanctity of their private property and their pockets. Relationships were not helped by the fact that the College Beadle's wages depended partly on nosing out and reporting suspect activity.

A physician in the shop of an apothecary (Photo Researchers, Inc/Alamy stock photo)

The barber-surgeons were marginally less respectable, professionally and socially, than the apothecaries. The Company of Barber-Surgeons was established in 1540 and it was both protected and controlled by the College. The College was able to prevent any formal recognition of the rights of surgeons to practise medicine, but they were obliged to grant *ad hominem* licences to allow surgeons limited rights to practise. The surgeons, however, were able to push against this in two main ways. Firstly, they were quick to co-opt the College's public health stance and argue that increasing the scope of their activities, particularly at times of war, was in the interests of the protection and health of the realm. The association of the surgeons with the army and the navy also meant that their company frequently attracted men with formal medical degrees, who tied their fortunes to armed service rather than to private practice. These factors made the surgeons marginally more impervious to the attempts to bring them to heel than the apothecaries.

The College's right to inspect [the apothecaries'] premises and then to burn drugs and other medicaments when found unsuitable directly attacked the sanctity of their private property and their pockets.

The irregular practitioners were a far more motley bunch and ranged from highly qualified foreign physicians who had not yet obtained a licence and men with bachelor's degrees in medicine to outright quacks and charlatans, as well an assortment of midwives, clergymen and servants.

The patterns of conflict between the other professions and the College can be seen in the very first attempt of the College to flex its regulatory muscle. In September 1525, Drs Bentley and Yaxley complained to the court about three men practising physic having 'no manner speculacion and cunnyng that to doo'.[15] While the surgeon Roys and the charlatan Westcott seem to have complied with the College's injunction to 'no more occupy physic', the apothecary Roger Smith was repeatedly pursued. The apparent failure to successfully prosecute Smith led the College to debate an application to Parliament to confirm and extend its privileges. While little came of this, it nonetheless set the pattern for future behaviour – the College would prosecute to the fullest possible extent, but when foiled, it would resort not just to have its authority confirmed by outside sources, but extended. The apothecaries were quick to cotton on to these tactics and they settled into a long legal and parliamentary battle with the College that was not fully resolved until the mid-nineteenth century.

In all, the College brought over 700 prosecutions in the period between 1550 and 1640. Which brings us to the question of why the College was so enthusiastic about regulation. It was far from easy, being reliant on the more senior members of the College taking time out of busy practices. In short, there is very little that bolsters professional self-confidence more than the politics of subordination and making much of minor differences in power and status.

THE COLLEGE AND PUBLIC HEALTH

The College had been conceived, at least in part, as a type of 'medical police', poised to intervene in the outbreak of plague then stalking England. Ironically, the intermittent outbreaks of plague served to weaken rather than strengthen the College. Although there is evidence of physicians going out among the citizens of London to give help, physicians tended to accompany their elite patients fleeing to the relative safety of the countryside. Not only did this interrupt College business, with too few fellows to make meetings quorate, but it drew sneers of derision from critics. Typically, the College would respond to this with a flurry of censorial activity, usually aimed at apothecaries and various irregular practitioners who, in retaliation, were painted as swindlers out to defraud a desperate populace by making false claims for their elixirs and tonics. Unfortunately for the College, the moral issue over the absence of the physicians was more convincing to the public than concerns over the effectiveness of treatments.

THE COLLEGE AND ITS INTELLECTUAL AGENDA

It was implicit at the time of its founding that the College was intended to serve as a shining beacon of the very best type of reformed Humanist medicine, imported from the most advanced medical school in Europe. However, the very early College made no provisions for publicly disseminating or promoting medical knowledge and the development of an intellectual programme within the College was surprisingly slow for an organisation that prided itself on learning.

The first gesture in the direction of educating fellows came in the form of a library. Linacre had donated books to the College at its founding and one of the two rooms at his house at Knightrider Street given over to the College was used as a small library, with the books kept in a chest. While Linacre's bequest to the College did include the library, the lion's share of his estate went to Oxford and Cambridge to provide permanent lectureships in medicine, on the grounds that the study of medicine was 'right mete and expedient for the then habitanntes in every comminalte to the comfort of the people and remedy of many maladies'.[16]

Unsurprisingly, it was Caius who began to pay more attention to the intellectual standing of the College and the education of its fellows. Caius had become an expert anatomist during his stay at Padua and he began to present at the Barber-Surgeons' hall shortly after his return. In 1565, the College obtained a grant to

Engraved for Chamberlain's History of London.

Wale delin.   *Grignion sculp.*

View of the manner of burying the dead Bodies
At Holy-well mount during the dreadful PLAGUE *in 1665*

Burying the dead during the dreadful plague in 1665

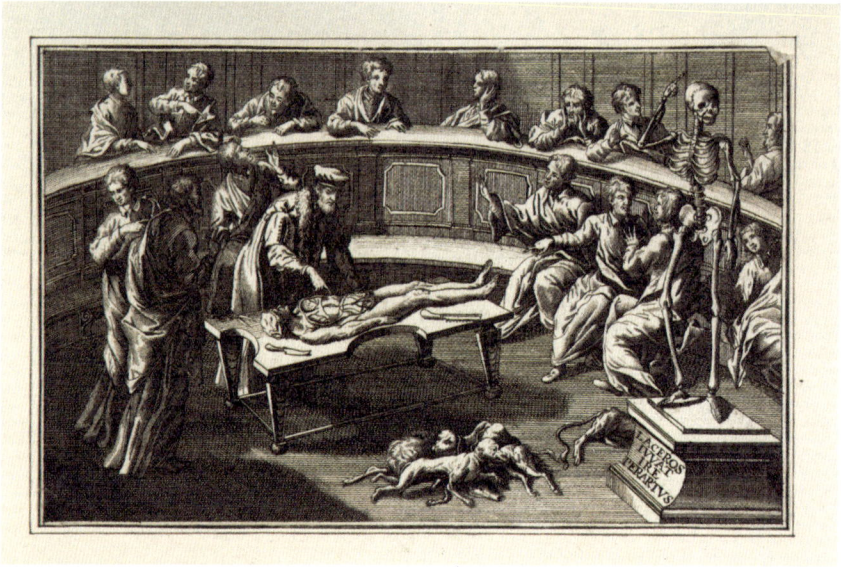

conduct its own public dissections using four corpses per year. The surgical theme continued with the founding of the Lumleian Lectures in 1582. John Lumley was a wealthy landowner with an extensive knowledge of anatomy. He had tried unsuccessfully to set up an endowment for anatomical teaching at the Barber-Surgeons' hall, but then turned to Richard Caldwell, a former College President. The stipend was substantial and the College so enthusiastic as to build a dedicated lecture theatre in which to hold the dissections. The first series of lectures was poorly attended, resulting in a decision that attendance was to be compulsory for all junior College members.

While there were signs of a nascent intellectual programme, the stuttering nature of this again drew criticisms of the College, although these would be markedly less wounding than comments about its failure as medical police.

TOP: An anatomical dissection in an anatomy theatre
MIDDLE: Detail from the Royal College of Physicians' charter for anatomies, letters patent by Elizabeth I, 1564
BOTTOM: Lord John Lumley

THE MEANING OF 'LEARNED'

As we have seen, the early College struggled to develop beyond an aggressively regulatory body, despite evidence that there were calls to do so from outside the College, and moves to do so from within. Instead, the College increasingly tightened its criteria for admission and was particularly obsessed by the issue of what level of medical knowledge was required for a physician to be considered suitably 'learned'.

The College was founded at the peak of the Humanist movement to reform the practice of medicine. The answer to the failures of physic to cure and comfort disease lay in reconstituting the perfect knowledge of the ancient Greeks through the better translation and interpretation of the texts of Galen and other medical authors. The degree of a physician's familiarity, then, with Humanist interpretations of Galen marked the extent to which he was versed in the most progressive medical knowledge of the time.

Most ironically, the idea of Galen as the pinnacle of medical learning was under threat within just a few years of the College's founding. In the universities, Humanism as an academic discipline was facing problems. It had gradually drifted from the endeavour to recover the original meaning of a text to the study of the text as an object in itself. The resulting mass of scholarship not only threatened to obscure the original texts themselves, but interfered with the ultimate, practical aim of Humanism, which was to inform right action in public life. It was under threat from other fronts

as well. The knowledge of the ancients had been thought to be perfect and infallible, yet this was demonstrated not to be true with the discovery of the New World. These concerns were to pale in the face of the Reformation, with its wholesale and systematic questioning and then attempted destruction of all forms of traditional authority.

At the same time, cracks were appearing in the façade of Galen's perfect knowledge of human anatomy. Andreas Vesalius had developed his own Humanist programme for the reform of medicine at the University of Padua. Unlike other scholars, who

ANDREÆ VESALII.

Portrait of Vesalius

INTEGRA ET   AB OMNIBVS

PARTIBVS   *LIBERA AC*
  nuda uenæ   *cauæ delineatio.*

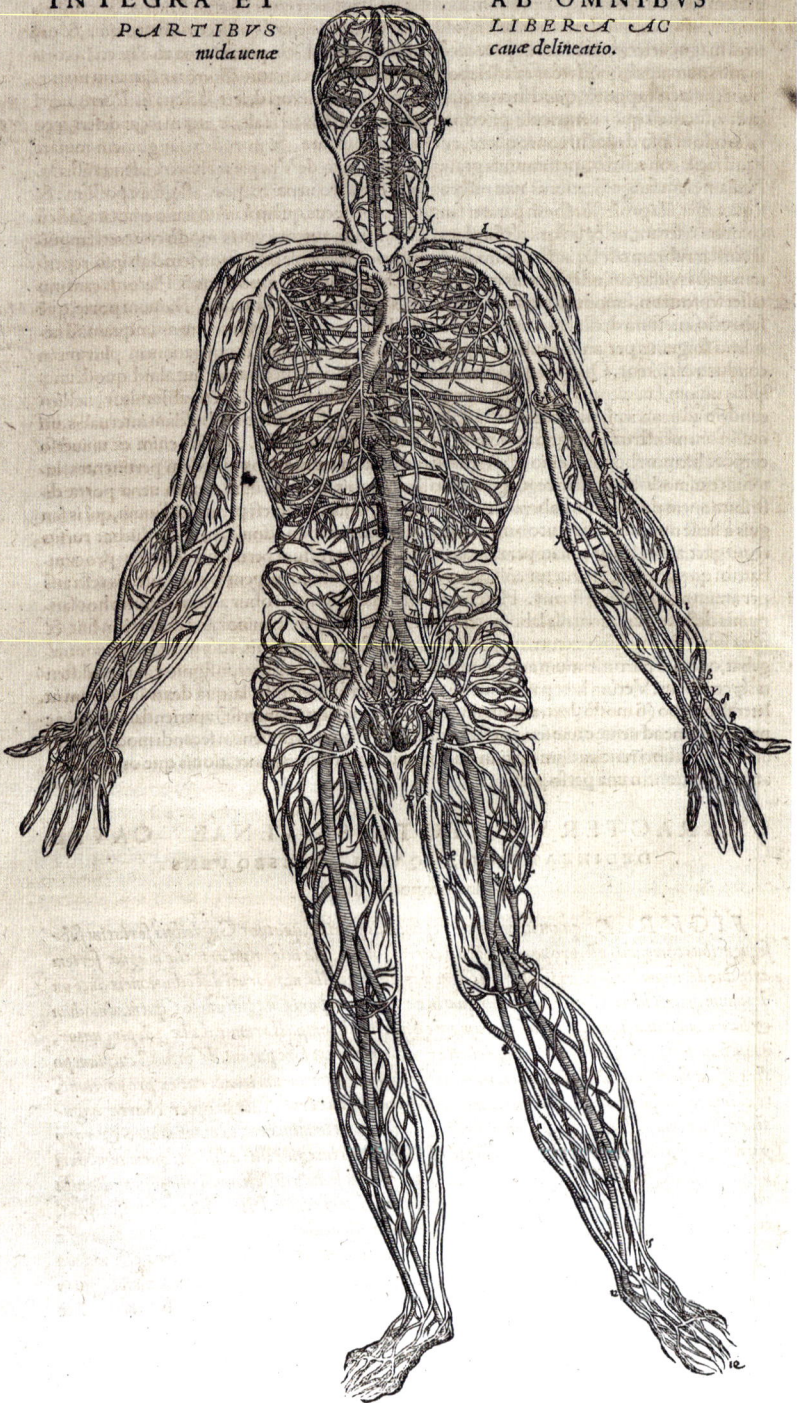

sought to create perfect texts, Vesalius was seeking to recreate a perfect anatomy, by following the precise rules laid out by Galen for dissection. To his surprise, Vesalius found marked differences between the bodies laid out on his table and the Galenic texts, forcing him to the conclusion that Galen had never dissected a human being, only Barbary apes. As a superior knowledge of anatomy was the keystone to Galen's theories of disease and healing, soon the whole structure started to crumble.

England was not such a backwater that the whole medical community could have been unaware of these developments. So it appears superficially absurd that the College, as a learned organisation, should shy away from progressive theories. However, the key point of differentiation of physicians from other medical practitioners lower down the scale was their university education, which equipped them to think in a highly sophisticated, 'philosophical' fashion, that is, like a learned man. So while the *theoria*, or general understanding of the physiological principles of the body and the causes of disease, was important, it was much less so than the *methodus medendi*, or the ability to manipulate information, in a way analogous to the philosophical rules of rhetoric, grammar and logic, to form a 'discourse of the state of the Disease'.[17]

The importance of the *methodus medendi* was captured in the College's system of examinations, which consisted of five rounds of questioning by the Censors, a number of fellows and the President. The first four rounds were highly choreographed. Each round dealt with a specific topic: medical theory

The key point of differentiation of physicians from other medical practitioners lower down the scale was their university education, which equipped them to think in a highly sophisticated, 'philosophical' fashion.

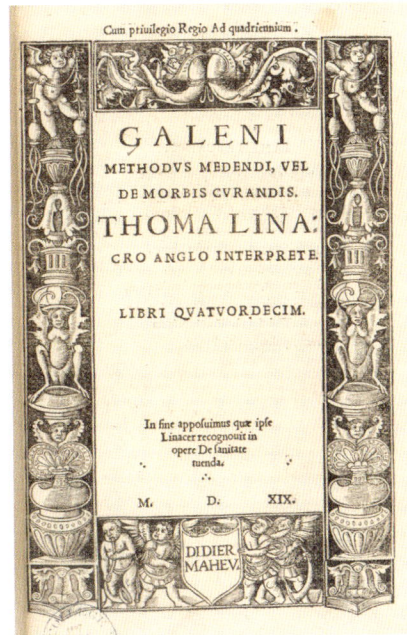

Cum priuilegio Regio Ad quadriennium.

GALENI
METHODVS MEDENDI, VEL
DE MORBIS CVRANDIS.

THOMA LINA:
CRO ANGLO INTERPRETE.

LIBRI QVATVORDECIM.

In fine appofuimus quæ ipfe
Linacer recognouit in
opere De fanitate
tuenda.

M.   D.   XIX.

DIDIER
MAHEV.

ABOVE: The title-page of Galen's *Methodus medendi* published in Paris, 1519
OPPOSITE: Anatomical figure in Vesalius' *De humani corporis fabrica*, published in 1543, page 268

(*speculatio*); the signs, causes and symptoms of disease (*semiotics*); methods of treatment; and, finally, the properties of healing substances (*materia medica*). The President would at random pick out three questions from different places in the texts prescribed by the College for that examination and show these to the candidate. The candidate would then be left alone with an index-free copy of Galen. After time for consideration, the candidate would then read out clearly his identification of passages of the text from which the questions were derived and give an account of his 'distinctions' in formulating answers. The fellows were to judge whether he had found the right places in the text, understood what he had read and reasoned his answers well. Any fellow could dispute points. The fifth part of the examination was the most important, as it was solely a test of the use and practice of medicine for which there were no set texts.

In their format, then, the College examinations were remarkably similar to the final university examinations of the time, which hinged on a series of disputations that aimed not just to assess textual knowledge of the writings of the authorities on any given subject, but rather to confirm that the student had acquired mastery over methods of philosophical reasoning. The College's examinations, then, were much less about a perfect knowledge of increasingly stale texts, but about testing whether a candidate could think about disease in a structured and professional manner.

The College's continued use of Galen as the ruler by which all physicians should be measured left it open to increasingly harsh criticism in the face of alternative theories of physiology and disease. Yet there is evidence that the College did soften on *theoria*, even while insisting on *methodus*. When in 1560 Dr Wendy Thomas accused John Geynes, an otherwise respectable member of the College, of 'shamelessly asserting to the vulgar that Galen had erred', Caius and the College found this utterly intolerable. Following a protracted series of escalating threats, including gaol, Geynes eventually capitulated and penitentially confessed his sins before the President and fellows. In contrast, a pass in the examinations later became contingent on the candidate demonstrating a reasonable level of medical knowledge and the ability to hold a rational discussion on disease and healing in a manner acceptable to the fellows.

The problem of 'learning' was also side-stepped in other ways. The example made of Geynes by Caius appears to have sent a distinct shudder through nearly a whole generation of physicians, and many turned away from scientific endeavours that might bring them into conflict with the College. Instead, they sought alternative ways of making themselves congenial to their high-ranking patients. One way was to comport themselves as gentlemen and to adopt the ornaments of the sophisticated man about town: 'his Library, Habit, his more free way of living in a suitable house, Attendants, greater Taxes, &c'.[18] The other was to display their intellectual qualifications through other pursuits aligned with the liberal arts, such as languages, theology and education. While these moves sought to minimise overt dissent, they created increasing tension between the notion of the physician as a sober and learned 'medical Bishop' and the desire of doctors to join the ranks of the gentry.

AN ASIDE ABOUT CAIUS, VESALIUS AND GALEN

Caius was far from unaware of the challenges to Galen's authority on matters of anatomy. Indeed, he had shared a house with Vesalius while in Padua. It has been postulated that Caius was so incensed by the temerity of Vesalius' programme that he went to academic war with his house-mate. Vesalius' offence was to privilege his own experience of anatomical dissection above all else and not to subordinate himself to the written text. Caius, on the other hand, continued to believe that a more perfect form of Galen could be recovered through philology, that is through better translations and close scrutiny of the original texts.

This casts an interesting light, then, on Caius's enthusiasm for anatomy within the College, his reputation as the finest of the early English anatomists and his privileging of Galen in the statutes. It opens up the possibility that Caius used his position within the College to subvert Vesalius on a grand scale. The rules he devised for the College inherently prohibited any physician from openly espousing Vesalius (or any other writer who cast doubt on Galen) without threat of ridicule, or worse. Moreover, Caius sought to exert an iron grip over the teaching of anatomy in London, both to the physicians and to the barber-surgeons. Did he actively seek to inoculate a whole nation of medical practitioners against the dangerous ideas of Vesalius? At the very least, he shifted the College from an organisation that viewed itself as being at the forefront of medical knowledge to one threatened and challenged by new developments.

A SUITABLE CANDIDATE?

The issue of the meaning of 'learned' was closely aligned with the problem of who was an appropriate person to be member of the College and participate in its business. As we have seen, the College was initially conceived as a quasi-egalitarian body, for which the only qualification for membership was a university medical degree. There was virtually no hierarchy and all fellows participated equally in the business of the College. However, as the restrictions on membership were increasingly tightened over the years, the College created new ranks of members with fewer privileges and lower status than the fellows.

The categories of 'candidate' and 'licentiate' seem to have come about more by accident than design. As the statutes set a maximum number of fellows, a physician on being successfully examined effectively had to join a waiting list for an empty seat, thereby becoming a 'candidate' of the College. During this time, the candidate was allowed to attend meetings, but not to vote. Later, the stipulation was added

The College created new ranks of members with fewer privileges and lower status than the fellows.

The categories of 'candidate' and 'licentiate' seem to have come about more by accident than design.

that candidates could only be eligible for fellowship after four years of practice, effectively expanding the pool even further. The term 'licentiate' first appeared in the annals in 1542. It was loosely used to describe physicians who held either an MD from a foreign university, an English MB or university licence and therefore still needed to submit themselves to examination by the College before they could have a licence to practise in London. The annals strongly imply that licentiates were initially able to vote in College elections and to hold office, activities from which they were later barred after admissions to the rank became more common in the 1580s. Insult was added to injury when the College began to levy double and triple the standard fees on licentiates.

The stipulation that fellows of the College must have medical degrees from Oxford or Cambridge and that only Englishmen could hold high office created an additional dimension of complexity. The statutes never included any specific comments with regard to religious affiliation. However, over the period of the Reformation and Counter-Reformation, most universities checked the confessional sympathies of their students. Oxford and Cambridge were no different and attendance at the

English universities became restricted to professing Anglicans. It was no longer sufficient to be 'learned' to be a fellow, one had to be Anglican. Men of all other religious persuasions, regardless of their learning, were effectively ghettoised and left languishing in the rank of licentiate.

These constraints, again, proved to be a major point of conflict. Foreign and other irregular physicians could often see little point in joining the College. Some on being summoned would submit – John Howell, who failed to incorporate his medical degree on time, had to pay a fine, promise to obey the President and give a College dinner. Others would only do so after pursuit, threats and the infliction of penalties. More vexing were the cases where an irregular physician was found not to be a suitable candidate, but then managed to procure the necessary qualifications with the help of powerful patrons. Although the number of fellows was periodically revised upwards, reaching thirty-four in 1618, they were increasingly outnumbered by the candidates and licentiates, and fully a quarter of all College members had at one time been pursued as an 'irregular'. This left the boundaries between the 'learned' fellows and everyone else increasingly blurred.

THE COLLEGE AND THE CROWN

The Tudor period also set the tone for the relationship between the College and the Crown. The foundation of the College had been dependent on the favour of a King, and it owed its authority directly to the Crown. These deep ties to the monarch meant that the College was a relative hostage to fortune and, as we have already seen, far more at the mercy of political and social turmoil than other more deeply embedded institutions, such as the universities or the guilds.

Moreover, as the College had freely made itself an instrument of the monarch's sacred duty to preserve and protect the people of England, there was a clear relationship between the reigning monarch's, and at times the government's, attitudes towards 'interventionist' policies and the activities of the College. At times when the Crown saw fit to intervene directly in the running of the realm, so the College responded with enthusiasm for prosecution and policing. This did mean, however, that the College was constantly looking to the monarch for support – any success that it had in obtaining further powers was contingent on the monarch's view of the College and his/her interest in harnessing learned bodies in the service of the realm.

The pattern of the College flourishing at times of more authoritarian government was discernible almost immediately after the founding of the College – it made a good start at the peak of Henry VIII's interest in enlightened rule, came to maturity during the reign of Mary and reached the height of its powers under the first two Stuarts. At other times, such as during the more turbulent periods of Henry's reign and that of Edward, or when the College was viewed as a something of an irrelevance, such as it was periodically by Elizabeth I, the College kept itself quiet and tended to 'dispose of its business in a sufficiently workmanlike way'[19] on the regulatory front.

The foundation of the College had been dependent on the favour of a King, and it owed its authority directly to the Crown.

King James I of England, also King James VI of Scotland (Wellcome Library, London)

THE POWER OF PATRONAGE

The relationship between the College and the Crown was usually mediated by one or two power-broking individuals in the College, who not only enjoyed the personal favours of the monarch, but were also able to exert considerable influence in the College. Linacre's relationship with Henry VIII, John Caius's with Mary I and Theodore de Mayerne's with successive Stuart kings are examples. Indeed, a valetudinarian turn of royal character tended to favour the College. So, for example, while Charles I had overcome rickets and other childhood ills to become a healthy adult, he nonetheless maintained a medical entourage of eight to ten doctors, alongside surgeons, apothecaries and a midwife. A small posse of physicians at the bedside was inclined to get the College's point across.

A number of royal physicians, however, stood outside of the rank and file of the fellows, the monarchs having penchants for either foreign physicians or borderline quacks, thereby creating problems for the College. Did they award the monarch's favourites with a fellowship, thereby acknowledging that the monarch had made an appropriate choice? Or did they insist on all physicians meeting the criteria contained in the statutes, risking the monarch's offence? Such questions caused the College much consternation. In some cases, the College was on solid enough ground. Worryingly for the College, Elizabeth I retained at her court several highly irregular practitioners, including the infamous alchemist John Dee and the occultist conjurer Edward Kelly, with whom Dee swapped wives. When the Queen asked, via Francis Walsingham in 1581, that her new favourite Margaret Kennix be allowed her 'small talent and craft',[20] the College politely demurred. In other cases, the College felt it more expedient to be as accommodating as possible. On James I bringing John Craige with him from Scotland in 1606, the College explicitly changed the statutes to allow 'British' MDs to join.

Despite the post of royal physician being the ultimate prize, the Crown was not the only valuable source of patronage. Indeed, patronage operated at almost every level in the medical marketplace as, to a certain extent, it replaced the usual community ties and natural networks of the guild structure. Having a rich and powerful patient was important, conferring a steady income, a degree of reflected status and the possibility of recommendations to others. But it was also important for the more junior physician to secure the interest and protection of more senior fellows. This was because upper-class patients were almost always attended by multiple physicians, with the lead doctor inviting second, third and occasionally fourth opinions from a small pool of trusted colleagues. Finding the approval of a senior physician could make a younger man starting out in the London; those who routinely offended their betters tended to find their careers over in virtually no time.

ABOVE: John Dee performing an experiment before Queen
Elizabeth I, oil painting by Henry Gillard Glindoni
(Wellcome Library, London)
RIGHT: John Dee

**Having a rich and powerful
patient was important,
conferring a steady income,
a degree of reflected
status and the possibility of
recommendations.**

STREET IN LONDON IN THE TIME OF MARY.

Street in London in the time of Queen Mary I (North Wind Picture Archives/Alamy stock photo)

THE COLLEGE, THE CROWN AND RELIGION

The putative neutrality of the College served it well in times of religious controversy and political upheaval. This is perhaps because the fellows, as a group, reflected the religious sentiments of learned English people generally – as the country shifted from Catholicism towards Anglicanism, so did the College. The College was also highly tactical and took care not to draw undue attention to itself at times of heightened sensitivities, as well as making moves to protect fellows from excessive scrutiny.

At the time of the founding of the College, there were only the very first rumblings of the religious strife to come; Martin Luther's Ninety-Five Theses, in which he outlined his objections to various Church practices, having been written only the year before. The College kept quiet during the first storms that accompanied Henry's ferocious quarrel with Rome, the founding of the Church of England and the dissolution of the monasteries. The College, however, continued to admit men who had made the increasingly perilous journey to Padua. While other universities in Europe were beset by the violence that accompanied the start of the Reformation in 1517, the Venetian Senate extended its protection to Protestant students. Padua made no necessity of confession of faith, yet English students were exposed to a form of Roman Catholicism that could no longer be practised in England.

The crypto-Catholic sympathies of the College came to the fore during Caius's presidency, which rapidly followed the accession of Mary in 1553. Mary's adviser Cardinal Pole had much in common with many of the senior fellows, including Caius. He had been tutored at Oxford by Linacre before attending Padua. The College and Caius benefited from the favour of Mary and Pole,

TOP: Queen Mary I (© National Portrait Gallery, London (4980 (16)))
ABOVE: Cardinal Pole (© National Trust Images, Hardwick Hall)

Queen Elizabeth I (© National Portrait Gallery, London (4449))

The outward neutrality of the College on religious matters served it well at the tricky juncture between the two Tudor queens. A number of fellows served as royal physicians at both Catholic and Protestant courts.

with both directly lending their strength to the College's regulatory activity and siding with it in periodic skirmishes with the universities. In return, as we have already seen, Caius recast the College as a form of 'medical clergy' and put itself into the hands of the monarch. By the end of Mary's reign, the College carried the distinct whiff of Popery.

Even by this time, however, the make-up of the College was beginning to change. The result of the College limiting fellowship to those with medical degrees from Oxford or Cambridge was to slow the rate of Englishmen attending at a continental university to a trickle, with only four of the twenty fellows admitted during Caius's presidency having studied abroad. The accession of Elizabeth I heralded a shift, as it did elsewhere, towards established Anglicanism.

The outward neutrality of the College on religious matters served it well at the tricky juncture between the two Tudor queens. A number of fellows served as royal physicians at both Catholic and Protestant courts. George Owen and Thomas Wendy were royal physicians to Henry VIII and Edward VI, as well as to the passionately Catholic Mary. Wendy lived long enough, and was seen to be so far above matters religious and political, that he served Elizabeth as well. Nor was Caius immediately defenestrated on Elizabeth's accession, continuing to serve as President for the first three years of her reign and remaining a royal physician until 1568. This neutrality also meant that, when attempts were made to ensure conformity within the College's ranks, the College was not further challenged when it stopped short of openly shopping those out of sympathy with the Queen and the government.

Still, there were sharp lessons for those who did not conform. Several members of the College were fined, imprisoned and even tortured for suspect beliefs and dubious activities. Others, including the former President Richard Smith, fled the capital. In 1594, Dr Roderigo Lopez,

Quid dabitis

Proditorum finis funis

Lopez compounding to poyson the Queene.

Roderigo Lopez

a converted Jew of Portuguese origin, was hanged, drawn and quartered for high treason. Nor did the College ever completely overcome suspicions that it was a secret hive of Popery, likely due in no small part to those fellows who defied specific laws against those who 'remain[ed] beyond the seas under the colour of study'[21] to study medicine at Padua.

By the time of the accession of James I, the College's membership was mainly conformist, although the religious orientation of the College was growing more diverse. This was not just because of the growing number of foreign dissenting physicians, but the growing influence of Calvinism in Cambridge. While this was advantageous to the College in some ways, in that it offered the possibility of change in times of shifting political and religious allegiances, it would become increasingly at odds with the inherent conservatism of the College.

THE COLLEGE DURING THE REIGN OF THE FIRST TWO STUARTS

King James I of England, also King James VI of Scotland (© National Portrait Gallery, London (548))

THE NEW REGIME

The tone of government entirely changed with the move of King James I from Scotland to London. Elizabeth was the last in the line of splendid Tudor regents and she had governed as a Renaissance Prince. In her decline, however, her court had become increasingly hierarchical, conventional and conservative. However, James's intellectual curiosity and dislike of ceremony meant that he was not entirely enthusiastic about the College, with its whiff of discipline and tradition, in the first years of his reign. As James took increasing interest in preserving the health of his nation, so the College again found itself aligned with the interest of the Crown. Keen to press its advantage, the College took every opportunity to expand its powers under the first two Stuarts.

As James took increasing interest in preserving the health of his nation, so the College again found itself aligned with the interest of the Crown.

THE COLLEGE VERSUS DR BONHAM

The revitalisation of the link between the authority of the monarch and the authority of the College can be seen in the case of Dr Bonham, a Cambridge-educated physician who had been practising in London for several years. Having initially associated with the barber-surgeons, he was refused admittance to the College fellowship in 1606. He was fined for practising without a licence, refused to pay the fine, was fined again and then eventually gaoled for contempt. Bonham's lawyer appealed on the grounds of *habeas corpus*, securing his release. The College sued again, with a counter-suit from Bonham for illegal trespass and illegal imprisonment. When the matter was finally heard before the Chief Justice, Sir Edward Coke, Bonham's lawyer exploited the gap between the College's original

Edward Coke (© National Portrait Gallery, London (D26085))

charter and the later statutes. He argued that the statutes had never intended to prohibit a university-educated man such as Bonham from practising, and disputed the College's right to control medical practice as a monopoly. Attention was drawn to the difference between 'malpractice', for which the College did have the ability to imprison a practitioner, and 'illicit practice', for which the stipulated punishment was a fine. Further, the College's charter did not permit it to judge Bonham's moral authority as a learned man. The College's defence borrowed heavily from the rhetoric of the Stuart monarchy and likened its authority to that of the King, which was required to restore and maintain the natural order. Like the King, who had the divine right to rule over his people, so the College had the right to judge the character, knowledge and behaviour of its members. Coke found in favour of Bonham, awarded him damages of £40 and issued the College with seven directions for future behaviour. Unhappy at this outcome, the College proceeded against the judgement by writ of error, which the King's Bench subsequently upheld. As the principles laid down by Coke were not overturned by the judgement, Bonham continued in his London practice, no longer harassed by the College.

The College's defence borrowed heavily from the rhetoric of the Stuart monarchy and likened its authority to that of the King.

The College's loss of the case on appeal came as something of a surprise to all concerned. Despite the loss, the argument remained that the King had a duty to govern the lives and health of all his subjects and the obligation to delegate his authority to agents acting on his behalf, it being impossible for the monarch to personally oversee all matters pertaining to the public good himself. In the matter of health, the College had the power, by way of its royal charter, to make laws governing the conduct of medical matters in the capital. It was some time before the College was challenged again on the matter of prosecuting irregular practitioners.

THE COLLEGE VERSUS THE APOTHECARIES

Having secured the support of the Crown, the College turned its attention to the perennial irritation of the apothecaries. As the College had been slow to consolidate its power over the apothecaries, it was eager to take advantage of James's favour and bring them more directly under its control.

From 1610, the College embarked on a campaign to separate the apothecaries from the Grocers' Guild with the promise of a new apothecaries' company. Although this ostensibly should have appealed to the apothecaries, the College planned to make

ffor the Tooth ach

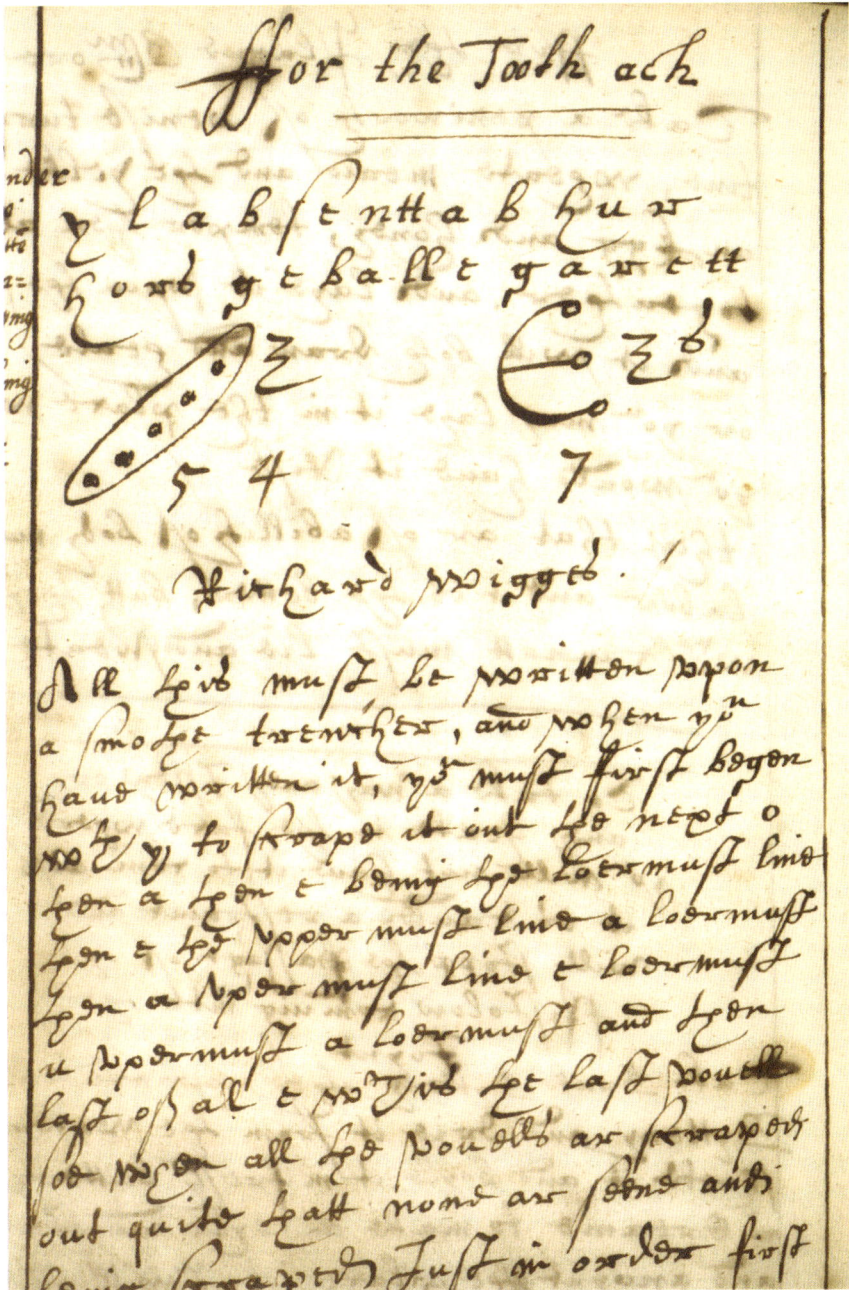

Sarah Wigges, *Hir booke* . . . 1616, p.283. Formally qualified doctors were rare and expensive. Instead, treatments were often prescribed and delivered by local 'healers' such as Sarah Wigges.

Apothecaries' Hall, Blackfriars Lane, London. The Worshipful Society of Apothecaries' first premises burnt down in the Fire of London. The society's new premises date from 1672 (Wellcome Library, London)

The apothecaries were no longer a small group, their numbers having grown rapidly during the expansion of London, and many were now men with wealth and connections.

the new company even more subordinate than the Grocers' had been. The royal physician, Theodore de Mayerne, and other senior College members persuaded James of the merits of the plan, yet the negotiations with the apothecaries proved lengthy, with the College making a number of key tactical errors. The apothecaries were no longer a small group, their numbers having grown rapidly during the expansion of London, and many were now men with wealth and connections. The College failed to fully appreciate how determined the apothecaries were to be independent, as well as underestimating the annoyance of the Grocers' Guild and the City of London, who resented the College's attempts to 'imminish'[22] their ancient liberties and authorities, as well as a lucrative revenue stream.

In 1617, the King created the Worshipful Society of Apothecaries by royal fiat. The final charter stipulated that the College was to continue to license all apothecaries, but no oath was prescribed to restrain apothecaries from the practice of medicine, nor were they limited any longer to dispensing prescriptions written by College members. For all the efforts of the College, the apothecaries now had the ability to administer medicines, a direct incursion into the College's own jealously guarded territory.

THE *PHARMACOPOEIA*

The idea of a *Pharmacopoeia*, which would constitute a definitive formulary for all physicians and apothecaries, was first floated in 1585. Being 'evidently a laborious undertaking',[23] its writing was deferred until the creation of the new Worshipful Society of Apothecaries spurred the College into action. The *Pharmacopoeia* was a mighty weapon dressed up as a book. As it was backed by a proclamation from the King, no one in England could compound or distil any substance except in the manner prescribed by the *Pharmacopoeia*. Nor could any substance not found in it be sold in London, upon pain of contempt.

The work involved was indeed prodigious. Fellows were asked to compose papers on items in the *materia medica*, which, after going through a committee process, were brought to be examined by the Registrar and the Elects. The process provoked much dissent. It was four years and four committees before a set of proofs could be assembled and then the initial publication was botched. The first edition was carelessly printed and full of mistakes. The College quickly withdrew it and a second edition appeared on 7 December 1618. The much-revised later edition contained an epilogue stating that the first edition had been published prematurely by the printer and without permission from the President. It has been suggested that the differences between the two volumes was a mark of the split between those fellows who wanted a relatively simple volume and those who wanted a much more elaborate and

ABOVE: *Pharmacopoeia Londinensis*, 1618, showing the royal command
OVERLEAF: *Pharmacopoeia Londinensis*, first edition 1618, showing pages 30–31

Pellitory of the wall [handwritten note]

Maluæ.
Helxines.
Pimpinellæ.
Plantaginis.
Adianthi albi & nigri ana. manipul. vnum.
Quatuor seminum frigidorum maiorum & minorum ana. drachmas tres.
Coquantur ex aquæ libris sex, *colatura* [handwritten] dum quatuor supersint, & cum
Sacchari albi libris quatuor.
Fiat Syrupus.

SYRVPVS DE ARTHEMISIA
MATHEI DE GRADI.

℞ Arthemisiæ manipul. duos.
Pulegij.
Calamenthi.
Origani.
Melissæ.
Persicariæ, siue Hydropiperis
Dictamni Cretici.
Sabinæ.
Sampsuchi. *Mariora* [handwritten]
Enulæ Campanæ.
Chamædryos. *Germander* [handwritten]
Perforatæ, i. Hyperici.
Chamæpithios.
Matricariæ cum flore.
Centaurij minoris.
Rutæ.
Betonicæ.
Buglossi ana. manipul. vnum.
Radic: Fœniculi.

Apij.
Petroselini.
Asparagi.
Rusci.
Saxifragiæ.
Enulæ.
Cyperi.
Rubiæ tinctorum.
Ireos.
Pœoniæ ana. vnciam nam.
Baccarum Iuniperi.
Sem: Leuistici.
Petroselini.
Apij.
Anisi.
Nigellæ.
Carpobalsami, siue Cubebarum.
Costi. *zedoary* [handwritten]
Radic: Asari.
Pyrethri.
Cassiæ ligneæ.
Cardamomi.
Calami aromatici.
Phu ana. vnciam dim diam.
Infundantur in sufficienti quant *libris duodec* [handwritten] tate aquæ per horas viginti quatuor, postea decoquantur ad me dietatis aquæ consumptionem, & tunc demittantur ab igne done aqua tepuerit, & postea colentur & colaturæ addatur mellis & sacchari quantum satis *ana libra duas* [handwritten], & propte viscositatem adde aceti acuti, ve scillitici magis vel minus secun dum quod placet, & fiat Syrupus &

& aromatizetur cum

Cinamomi & Spicæ ana. drach-
mis tribus.

SYRVPVS AVGVSTANVS VEL DE RHABARBARO AVGVSTANORVM.

℞ Rhabarbari optimi, vncias duas semis.

Foliorum, senæ, vnciam vnam
semis.

Florum violarum, manipul. v-
num.

Cinnamomi drachmam vnam
semis.

Zinziberis drachmam dimi-
diam.

Aquarum Betonicæ.

Cichorij.

Buglossi ana. libram
vnam.

Infundantur per noctem, colatura mane facta, decoquantur in
syrupum cum

Sacchari electi, libra vna semis,
addendo.

Syrupi rosati solutiui compo-
siti, vncias quatuor.

SYRVPVS ROSATVS SO-LVTIVVS SINE HEL-LEBORO.

℞ Myrobalonorum omnium ana.
vncias duas.

Contundantur crasso modo &
infundantur in libris quindecim

infusionis rosarum horis viginti
quatuor, cui adde

Radicum Polypodij vncias duas semis.

Semin: Carthami vnciam vná *bastard saffron*
semis.

Semin: Anisi.

Fœniculi ana. drachmas sex.

Foliorum Senæ vncias tres.

Epithymi vnciam vnam semis.

Corticum citri vnciam vnam.

Cariophyllorum vnciam di-
midiam.

Nucis Moschatæ drachmas tres.

Fiat rursus infusio horis viginti
quatuor, quibus elapsis, fortissima
fiat expressio, & adde ad liquoris
singulas libras duas.

Sacchari libram vnam.

Fiat syrupus. Et hic ingreditur
compositionem Syrupi Augusta-
norum, vel de Rhabarbaro solutiui.

SYRVPVS DE CICHORIO CVM RHABARBARO.

℞ Hordei integri.

Radic. Apij.

Fœniculi.

Asparagi ana. vncias
duas.

Cichorij.

Taraxaconis, i. dentis leonis. *Dandelion*

Endiuiæ.

Cicerbitæ seu Souchi læuis ana. *sowthistle*
manipul. duos.

Lactucæ

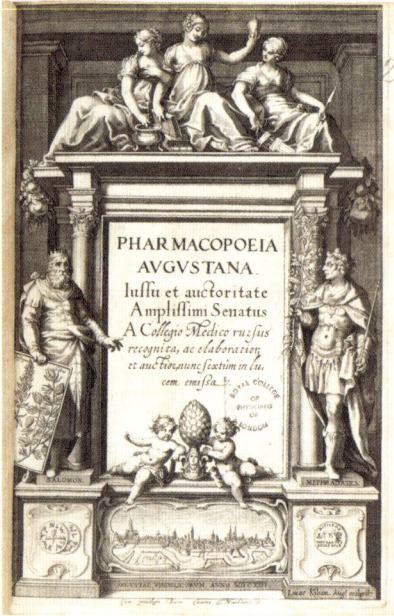

Title-page of the *Pharmacopoeia Augustana*,
Augsburg, 1613

The *Pharmacopoeia* could be considered to be the first large-scale collaborative project undertaken by the College and the first step in revitalising the College's languishing intellectual programme.

scholarly production. Other scholars have pointed to the highly suspicious similarities between the London *Pharmacopoeia* and the *Pharmacopoeia Augustana*, published in Augsburg in 1613, raising the possibility that the committee did not remotely follow the procedure agreed and had attempted plagiarism on a grand scale instead. In any case, its publication met with success, with the *Pharmacopoeia* going through another nine editions over the next century. While the first edition(s) are more notable for their seemingly bizarre ingredients, such as urine of a goat (for deafness), viper fat, powdered mummy and moss from a human skull, later editions were more rigorous in removing outdated and inefficacious remedies.

The *Pharmacopoeia* could be considered to be the first large-scale collaborative project undertaken by the College and the first step in revitalising the College's languishing intellectual programme. Moreover, it gave candidates and junior fellows an opportunity to participate in the business of the College in a way unrestricted by rigid hierarchy, as all fellows were allowed to submit papers. The *Pharmacopoeia* demonstrated how intellectual activities might bond the fellows into a corporate professional body and it also pointed the way to how patronage relationships might be renegotiated – a younger doctor lacking connections could come to the attention of his older colleagues and potentially powerful patients through a display of intellect, while at the same time contributing to the collective prestige of the College. It had taken the College a century to find a project that reflected, if only in part, its Humanist origins.

THE COLLEGE AS MEDICAL POLICE

As well as taking on the irregulars and the apothecaries, the College once more turned its hand to matters of public health as a way of expanding its empire. Plague policy in Stuart England rested in the hands of the Privy Council, which dictated actions to local government, who were expected to put in place quarantines and other public health measures. The City of London had made half-hearted attempts to involve the College in managing plague outbreaks between 1578 and 1625. These were not fruitful, with the City ignoring the advice of the College and relationships likely being marred by the City's involvement in the ongoing war with the apothecaries. When the next epidemic threatened in 1630, Charles I asked the College to help the Crown to take matters more directly in hand and the College responded enthusiastically.

'Necessary Directions, as well for the cure of the Plague, as for preventing the Infection',[24] however, proved a difficult undertaking, with the College submitting a short tract several weeks after the deadline. The College's proposals, rather than providing a cure for the plague, focused far more on prevention and drew attention to the issues of overcrowding, poor housing and inadequate sewerage. When later taken to task for the inadequacy of their proposals at combating plague, the College was able to point to the deficiencies of the City of London in executing their plans. This proved a winning tactic and it was one that the College repeatedly used for each plague outbreak thereafter. It demonstrated the

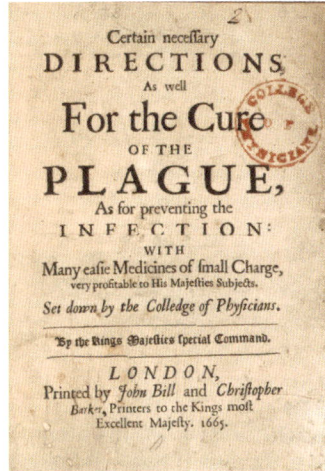

Certain necessary directions for the cure of plague, published in London, 1665

College to be learned and cooperative, but effectively shielded it from criticism.

Theodore de Mayerne, Charles' royal physician and a leading member of the College, had more ambitious plans. He proposed the formation of a board of health, into which the 'police' powers of the City of London would be placed. Led by members of the College, the board would have absolute authority to decree and enforce any measures seen necessary to improve public health.

The proposals for the health board were never approved by the Privy Council, although plans pressed ahead to make the City of London more accountable for the imposition of quarantine and other measures during future outbreaks of plague. These, too, fell through with the increasing schism between the King and Parliament.

AN ASIDE ABOUT AMEN CORNER

The premises on Knightrider Street, left by Linacre to the College, were sufficient to house the handful of original College members. However, the growth of the College led to increasing crowding of its two small rooms. In the 1580s, an anatomy theatre was added to accommodate the Lumleian Lectures. This was still not sufficient and the College began to seek alternative premises. Contributions from Lady Arabella Stuart and her aunt, the Countess of Shrewsbury, both of whom were imprisoned in the Tower of London at the time, bolstered the College's coffers. A property at Amen Corner, Paternoster Row, very near Knightrider Street, was leased from St Paul's Cathedral. The new house was large enough to provide a meeting room, a library, two rooms for anatomy and accommodation for a resident fellow, whose job it was to guard the property. The College moved into its new premises in August 1614.

Amen Corner, former home of the Royal College of Physicians

Theodore de Mayerne

AN ASIDE ABOUT THEODORE DE MAYERNE

The changing nature of the College and 'the doctor' over the period of the early Stuarts is captured in perhaps the most distinguished physician of the age, Theodore de Mayerne. De Mayerne embodied almost everything that Caius had tried so hard to regulate against. To begin with, he was not English and his education was bitty. His Huguenot family had fled Lyon to Switzerland following the St Bartholomew's Day massacre of 1572. He flitted about the Continent from Geneva to Heidelberg and then to Montpellier, where he finally graduated. Coming to London after years at the French Court to become royal physician to James I and his queen, he was showy, exotic and reeked of heterodoxy. He was a dissenting Protestant at a court

Members of the College were not just tolerant of de Mayerne, as they often were of flashy court physicians. They were in awe.

increasingly sympathetic to Catholicism, a fierce critic of Galen, and one of the first physicians to openly advocate Paracelsian 'chemical medicine'. He seems to have practised as an irregular physician for his first ten years in London, not seeking to become a fellow until 1616. He was as far as possible from being the 'profound, sad and discreet' doctor described as ideal in the act.

Yet members of the College were not just tolerant of de Mayerne, as they often were of flashy court physicians, they were in awe. When he was finally proposed as a fellow, he was unanimously elected, and an extraordinary committee meeting was convened solely for the purpose of his admission to the College. He rapidly became a leading light in the College, spearheading the *Pharmacopoeia* and 'medical police' projects and suggesting the new Worshipful Society of Apothecaries. Despite this, he demurred when offered the post of President, citing his many other interests as an impediment.

While de Mayerne was a man of unusual talent, he points to the ways in which the notion and status of the doctor was changing. In the first instance, there were markedly more of them. While the number of fellows had grown slowly over the first hundred years of the College, it increased the limit for the number of fellows five times over the next eighty years, from twenty-seven to eighty by 1687. This growth in the number of doctors was fuelled by a population explosion in the City of London and the concomitant rise of the 'middling classes', to which the physicians, regardless of pretensions to gentlemanliness, belonged. The result was an increasing heterogeneity in the educations, religious and political persuasions and opinions of College members. Moreover, the great prizes of wealth and status were available only to a select few, opening a widening gap between those at the top of their game and the rank and file – an irony at a time when doctors were finally becoming more professionally and socially secure.

Sir Charles Scarburgh, a learned physician. He is shown with a volume of Vesalius, a globe and a view of Rome in the background. Scarburgh was educated at Cambridge and became physician to King Charles II. He was one of the first fellows of the Royal Society

THE COLLEGE FROM CIVIL WAR TO CROMWELL

Eve of the battle of Edge Hill (Courtesy of National Museums Liverpool, Walker Art Gallery)

King Charles I giving orders to Sir Edward Walker (Wellcome Library, London)

As an organisation that directly derived its authority from the reigning monarch, the conflicts between King and Parliament and the rapid shifts in where real power lay posed existential threats to the College.

'AN END TO MANNERS'

After a relatively long period of stable government, from Elizabeth through to James, the coming to the throne of Charles I in 1625 marked the start of a period of political turmoil. In the space of just over half a century, the King attempted to rule without the consent of Parliament, a civil war was fought, the reigning monarch was beheaded, a republic was established and then dissolved and a monarchy was restored and then overthrown in a bloodless 'glorious Revolution'. This 'world turned upside down' was accompanied by profound social, political and cultural changes that touched on the lives of every English man, woman and child. It was also in this extraordinary period that the 'new philosophy' of Francis Bacon sparked developments in virtually all disciplines of scientific endeavour – mathematics, physics, chemistry, astronomy, biology.

Unsurprisingly, this exacerbated the tensions already simmering away in the College which became only more marked as England descended into turmoil and civil war. The perceived weakening of the authority of the College led to the development of rival organisations, focusing the more nebulous intermittent criticisms of the College into direct challenges. As an organisation that directly derived its authority from the reigning monarch, the conflicts between King and Parliament and the rapid shifts in where real power lay posed existential threats to the College. The extent of this can be seen by the College reducing its regulatory activity in the 1630s and then ceasing altogether for a period of nearly thirty years. The College stopped fighting with the irregular practitioners and the apothecaries, and instead started fighting for its survival. In this, the College displayed a remarkable degree of opportunism in its multiple changes of leadership and policy, seeking to align itself rapidly with whoever was in the ascendant. It also sought to quietly bolster its reputation by paying more attention to its intellectual programme.

THE COLLEGE AND THE CIVIL WAR

The College had actively sought to align itself with Charles I during the first years of his reign. The attempts to form a board of health were rewarded with support for the College when the Worshipful Society of Apothecaries fired off yet another salvo against the College. By way of retaliation, de Mayerne rapidly obtained a patent for a new Company of Distillers in 1638, hitting the Apothecaries right in their pocket-books. By 1640, Parliament and the King were increasingly at odds and the Apothecaries shifted tactics, openly cultivating Parliament. Caught on the back foot, the College swiftly realised that the traditional appeal to the monarch would no longer be a winning play. It began to distance itself from the monarchy, allowing increasing compromises on whether to seek support from the King, Parliament or the House of Lords to reinforce its authority as the 'sole and primary judges of physicians and physic and medicine and makers and compounders thereof in and near to the City of London'.[25]

King Charles I is seized by Cornet Joyce
(Wellcome Library, London)

By 1641, the College had to choose between the King and Parliament and, in October 1641, it declared itself for Parliament.

By 1641, the College had to choose between the King and Parliament and, in October 1641, it declared itself for Parliament by electing an entirely new set of leaders. For a time, there were nine Elects instead of the usual eight, underlining the radical shift in the College's outward politics. Parliament, however, was suspicious of an organisation that had touted itself as an agent of the authority of the monarch. Reluctant to draw more attention to itself following the outbreak of the Civil War, the College ceased virtually all regulatory activity in 1642. The descent into chaos of England was mirrored within the College. Meetings were poorly attended and the cessation of regulation meant that the College had virtually no income. Factional splits were rife, as the College increasingly flip-flopped between Royalist and Parliamentarian leadership, depending on who looked like they might have the upper hand. The College was heading towards possible extinction.

NEW CRITICS OF THE COLLEGE

The weakness of the College was seized upon by new opponents. The Puritans were once considered a small, radical fringe of Calvinism, who sought to 'purify' the Anglican Church of any remnants of superstitious Roman Catholic beliefs. However, the increasing sympathies of James I and Charles I with Catholicism transformed the Puritans into the main opposition party of the Civil War. Like the Humanists before them, the Puritans believed that it was possible to create a new future, based on historical and biblical ideals, through the efforts of human intellect and labour. The growing perception that the classics were ultimately pagan in their origins repelled them and they turned instead to the reformed knowledge of Francis Bacon and other English writers, such as Samuel Hartlib, to guidance in building a 'New Jerusalem' or Garden of Eden on earth.

Bacon had been acutely aware of the flaws in the Humanist and Scholastic programmes and conceived of an audacious plan for the 'Great Instauration', or renewal of all learning. In two books, *The Advancement of Learning* of 1605 and *Novum Organum Scientiarum* ('New Instrument of Science') of 1620, Bacon laid out the foundations of a 'new philosophy', along with a method of 'true directions' which would advance natural knowledge in all regions of possible discovery and lead to the domination of nature for the 'relief of man's estate'. At the heart of Bacon's new philosophy was the application of inductive reasoning, the making of generalisations from observations. He described a process of making careful, systematic observations in order to construct 'natural histories', which would allow the generalisation of a set of facts into one or more axioms. Testing of the axioms either through further observation or experimentation allowed them to be refuted or refined, with the establishment of more precise axioms. The whole process is then repeated in a step-wise fashion to build an increasingly complex knowledge of the world, one robustly supported by observed, empirical data. Bacon's position within the courts

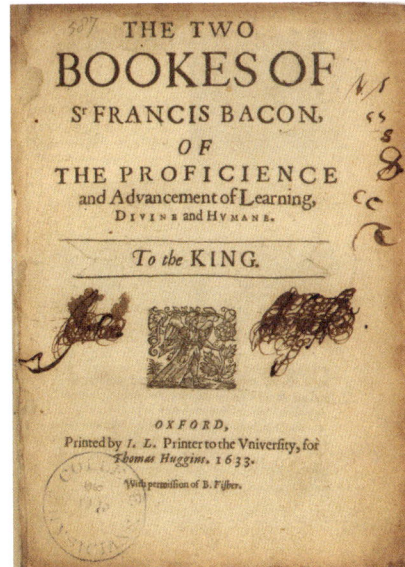

TOP: Francis Bacon
ABOVE: Title-page of *The two bookes of Sir Francis Bacon,* Oxford 1633

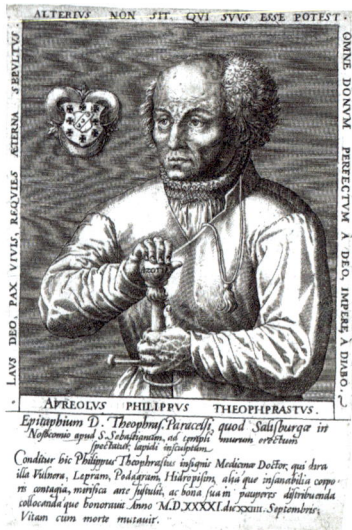

Paracelsus

of Elizabeth I and James I ensured that his ideas found a wide audience. However, it was not until the Civil War that his ideas were most enthusiastically seized upon and put to work furthering the Puritan cause.

A number of Puritans also saw hope for medical reform in the works of Swiss physician Paracelsus. The appeal of Paracelsus was two-fold. Firstly, he rejected the conventional Galenic *materia medica*, instead championing the use of 'chemical remedies' based primarily on sulphur, mercury and salt. Secondly, he sought to fashion a method of medicine with a Christian basis, offering a viable alternative to the pagan and base knowledge of the ancient Greeks. Paracelsus' notion that disease was a reflection of man's fall from grace and that the role of healer was to imitate Christ by paying attention to bodily and spiritual needs was almost directly analogous to the Puritan mission to restore mankind to perfect harmony with God.

Medical reform was a subject close to the hearts of the Puritans because of its potential ability to relieve suffering and improve the ability of men to build the New Jerusalem. The College's adherence to Galen and its monopolistic hold on the medical profession were major impediments to the Puritans' programme. The physicians were further charged with failing to aid the sick and poor, preferring instead to pander to their rich patients and fill their own pockets. Not content with waging an increasingly vigorous pamphlet campaign against the College, the medical reformers made a number of attempts to construct alternative colleges. William Rand's proposals for a College of Graduate Physicians consisting of 'more studious, public and humble spirited' practitioners in the mid-1650s did not get far.[20] The Society of Chemical Physicians, a group of pro-Paracelsian physicians, apothecaries and surgeons, did begin to meet on a regular basis and attracted a number of influential supporters. However, the heterogeneity of its membership, supposedly one of its strong points, rapidly led to internal infighting and the collapse of the Society.

Not content with waging an increasingly vigorous pamphlet campaign against the College, the medical reformers made a number of attempts to construct alternative colleges.

AN ASIDE ABOUT NICHOLAS CULPEPER

Of all the critics of the College, Nicholas Culpeper was perhaps the most ferocious. A Cambridge-educated apothecary, Culpeper freely practised a radical form of astrological medicine from a shop in Spitalfields, treating many of his poorer patients for free. He fervently believed in the providence of God, who freely provided herbs and other simples for the cure of disease. Moreover, he was convinced that the hierarchical structures of medicine were akin to those of the monarchy and Roman Catholic Church, designed to hoard power and money while restricting the freedoms of men.

The outbreak of the Civil War and the College's inability to police medical publishing provided Culpeper with an opportunity to go more directly on the offensive against the College. In 1649, he published *A Physical Directory*, an English translation of the *Pharmacopoeia* from the original Latin, supplemented with lists of herbs and other simples. The foreword sharply admonished the College for behaving like the papists and refusing the common man access to knowledge through the use of Latin.

The College was incensed. Culpeper had made the trade secrets of the College available to the public, undermining its authority. Yet the ire and outrage of the College and its royalist supporters mattered little to Culpeper – *A Physical Directory* was wildly

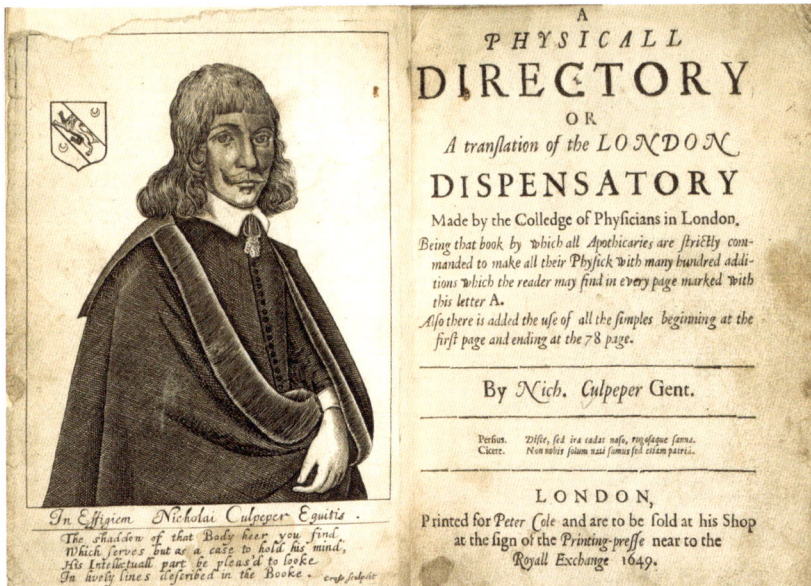

Frontispiece and title page of Culpeper's *A Physical Directory* … London 1649

successful with the public. Three more editions went to print in the next few years, each with stinging prefaces accusing the College variously of being an inefficient monopoly, motivated by financial self-interest, ignoring academic progress and intellectual conspiracy. As it was doubtful that Culpeper had broken any laws and, in any case, no legal action could be taken, the College was unable to issue any formal rebuke or stem the torrent of Culpeper's other medical works. Relief from Culpeper's onslaught came only with his untimely death in 1654, after which the College set about destroying his posthumous reputation, reducing him to an ignorant charlatan.

WILLIAM HARVEY SHOWS THE WAY

The College was painfully aware of the existential threats from both within and without. Yet it took several years for the College to begin to recast its purpose, give physicians a reason to be become members and ensure its survival.

Ironically, one of the things that threatened the College, the new philosophy, was the thing that saved it from extinction. Although the new philosophy had been enthusiastically enfolded into the rhetorical armamentarium of the Puritans, a number of Royalist physicians and intellectuals tentatively at first, and then with greater boldness, began to co-opt aspects of it to create their own reformed medicine, one based on a revised system of anatomical Galenism. In England, the lead was taken from medical researchers, such as Franciscus de la Böe Sylvius and Marin Mersenne, working on the Continent, where the new philosophy was not tainted with Puritan associations. Mersenne was particularly influential, with many Royalists residing in Paris, such as Kenelm Digby, Thomas Hobbes and William Cavendish, working directly with the Mersenne circle.

The clearest expression of how the new philosophy might be used to bolster Galenic medicine and build a bulwark between the learned men of the College and the empirics who appealed to experimentation and experience was to be found closer to home in the form of William Harvey. Harvey had studied at Padua and, like Caius before him, had been entirely struck by the form of anatomy taught there. His teacher Professor Girolamo Fabrici d'Acquapendente, better known as Fabricius, had been in the midst of an ambitious programme of anatomical research. He was determined to resurrect Aristotle's anatomical practice and to thereby locate that which had eluded Aristotle –

ABOVE: Doctor of Medicine diploma from the University of Padua to William Harvey, 1602
OVERLEAF: Illustration from Harvey's *De motu cordis*, 1628

Harvey's detailed experiments with the valves of the aorta and veins led him inexorably to the conclusion that the blood must circulate through the body and lungs.

enim satis sua sponte, è maioribus in minores ramulas intrudi, è massa
& fonte separari, aut è locis calidioribus in frigidiora migrare ; verisi-
milius est)Sed omnino valuulæ factæ sunt, ne à venis magnis in minores moueretur sanguis & sic illas dilaceraret, aut varias cosas efficeret,
neue à centro corporis in extrema: sed potius ab extremitatibus ad cé-
trum progrederetur , ita huic motui valuulæ tenues facile recluduntur-
tur, cótrarium omnino supprimunt, & sic positæ & ordinatæ vt si quid
per cornua superiorum minus prohiberetur transitu , sed quasi per ri-
mas elaberetur conuexitas subsequentium transuersim posita excipe-
ret, & sisteret ne vlterius transiret.

Ego illud sæpissime in dissectione venarum expertus sum, si à radice
venarum initio facto, versus exiles venarum ramosSpicillum mitterem
(quanto potuerim artificio) ob impedimentum valuularum longius
impellere, non potuisse:contra vero forinsecus è ramulis radicem versus facillime , & pluribus in locis valuulæ binæ ad inuicem ita positæ,
& aptatæ, vt ad amussim (dum eleuantur) in media venæ cauitate co-
hæreant & vniantur, extremitatibus conuexis inuicem ; vt neque visu,
cernere, neque satis explorare rimulam aut coitum liceret, contra vero
forinsecus intro immisso stylo cedunt, & (valuularum, quibus cursus
fluminum inhibentur in morem)facillime reclinantur, vt motum sanguinis profectum à corde, & vena caua intercipiant, & ad amussim pluribus in locis elébat inuicem dum clauduntur , omnino inhibeant &
supprimant, & siue sursum ad caput, siue deorsum ad pedes, siue ad late-
ra brachii sanguinem à corde moueri(ita sunt constitutæ) vt nusquam
sinant, sed motui omni sanguinis qui à maioribus venis auspicatus, in
minores desinat, aduersentur & obsistant : ei vero qui à venis exili-
bus incipiens in maiores desinat , obsecundent liberamque & pa-
tentem viam expediant.

Sed quo veritas hæc apertius elucescat; ligetur brachium supra cu-
bitum viuo homine, tanquam ad mittendum sanguinem A A per in-
terualla apparebunt , præcipue in rusticis & varicosis, tanquam nodi
quidam & tubercula B.C.D.D.E.F. non solum vbi est diuaricatio E. F.
sed etiam vbi nulla [C.D.] & isti nodi à valuulis fiunt. Hoc modo ap-
parentibus in exteriori parte manus vel cubiti si à nodo inferius polli-
ce vel digito comprimendo sanguinem, & de nodo illo siue valuula
detraxeris] H. 2. figur.]videbis nullum (inhibente omnino valuula)
subsequi posse & venæ portionem (H. O. secúdæ fig.)infra tuberculú
& digi-

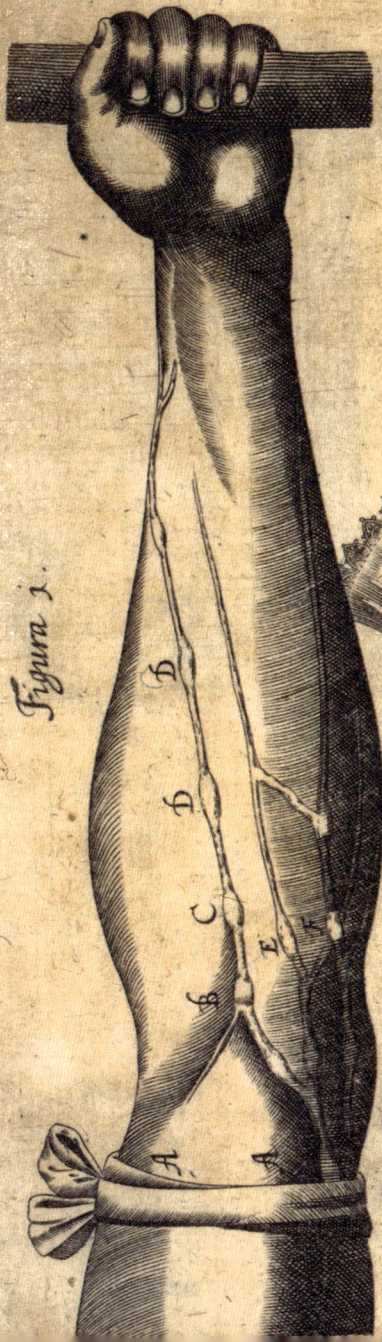

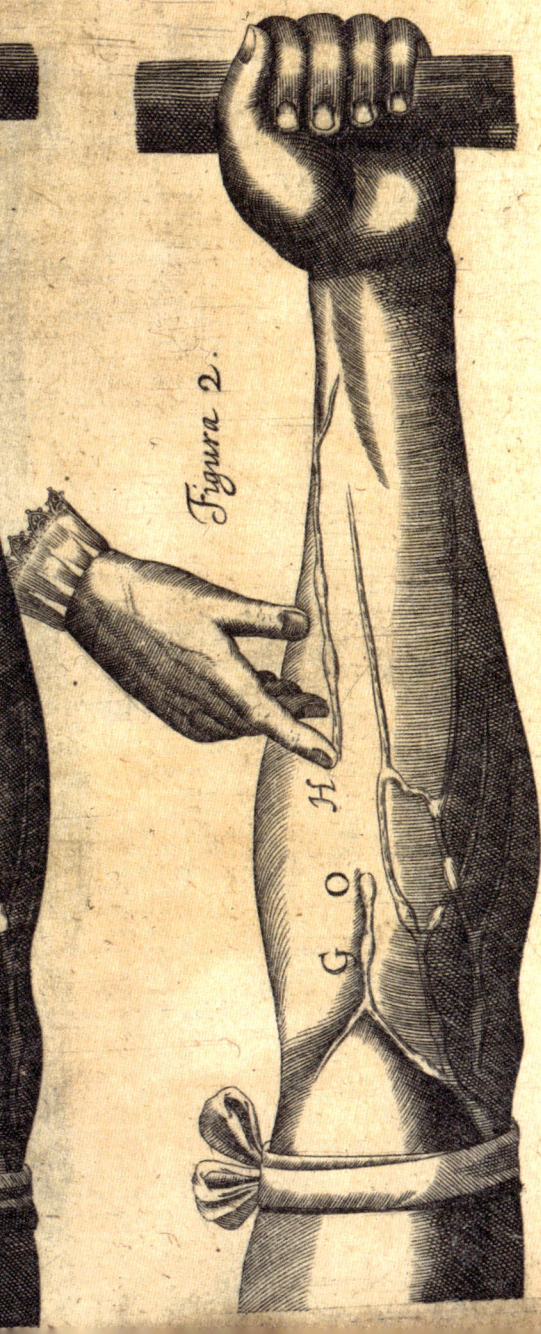

the seat of the soul. On his return to England, Harvey embarked on his own project. His task was to investigate the only anatomical topic left untouched by his teacher, the actions of the heart and circulation, in order to come to a universal understanding of the Aristotelian 'vegetative soul'. This focus on a very specific anatomical topic led him to vivisect scores of different animals, in addition to undertaking detailed human dissections, and allowed a number of key observations missed by earlier researchers. His finding, for example, that the amount of blood pumped by the heart each day was in excess of 500 pounds led him to the conclusion that the traditionally held notion that the liver continuously produced blood, which was then distributed to the peripheral tissues by the heart and then absorbed, was not physically possible. Similarly, his detailed experiments with the valves of the aorta and veins led him inexorably to the conclusion that the blood must circulate through the body and lungs.

Contrary to the commonly held notion, Harvey's conclusions were not instantly heralded as the greatest discovery in all of medical history. Instead, he was deeply unhappy with the implications of his research. Rather than resurrecting a purer and better form of ancient medicine, he had destroyed its central physiological tenets:

> *those things [...] are so new and unheard of, that not only do I fear harm to myself from other people's ill-will, but I likewise fear that every man will be my enemy, so much does custom and doctrine once received and deeply rooted prevail with everyone.*[27]

As he feared, his patients abandoned him following the publication of *De motu cordis* in 1628. He fared better with his fellow physicians and his patron, being re-elected as a Censor of the College in 1629 and retaining the favour of Charles I. However, by the start of the Civil War, his findings had failed to make any major difference to the traditional practice of Galenic medicine. He followed the King to Oxford, rapidly settling back into intense academic pursuits.

The remaking of the reputation of Harvey began in the mid-1640s. With little to do in the face of the Civil War, a group of younger London physicians, later known as the 1645 Group, began to meet to discuss the new philosophy. While Baconian natural philosophy still represented a threat to the College, the adoption of Harvey's experimental philosophy did not, as it combined detailed knowledge of the classical authors with new approaches to comparative anatomy. It contained just enough of the old philosophy to reinforce its learned nature, while embracing just enough observation and experimentation to make it 'modern'. Moreover, the true radical nature of Harvey's discoveries could be brushed aside by making his method an improvement on, rather than a refutation of, Galen. This way, there was no threat to the *methodus medendi* essential to the authority of the learned physician, nor was there any necessity to radically change the scope of the *materia medica*.

AN ASIDE ABOUT THE ANATOMICAL TABLES

Six remarkable anatomical tables currently reside in the College. Each of the six tables is 6'3" long and 30" wide, and displays a different part of the human body – arteries, veins and nerves – dissected out and mounted under coats of varnish. There are only two sets of such tables still in existence – our own being one set, the other set of four being in the Hunterian Museum of the Royal College of Surgeons, and they are thought to represent some of the oldest surviving anatomical specimens in Europe. Both sets originated in Padua. The precise origins of the College set are unknown, but the diarist John Evelyn purchased the set at the Hunterian Museum from the Italian anatomist Giovanni Leoni. While it is possible that Leoni also created the College's set, it is also possible that they were the work of their first owner, John Finch. Finch met Sir Thomas Baines while at Cambridge and the two soon became inseparable. They went to Italy in 1651 to study medicine at Padua and remained in Italy for over twenty years, with Finch eventually becoming professor of anatomy at the University of Pisa. Finch had not yet arrived in Padua at the time of the creation of Evelyn's tables in 1646, yet it remains plausible that he may have seen or picked up the technique from Leoni during his anatomical studies there.

John Evelyn was a man of an antiquarian bent rather than being a doctor or an experimental natural philosopher. That he should have gone to so much trouble to purchase and then ship such fragile objects back to England is a testimony to the impact that Harvey's discoveries had on the notion of what was considered to constitute important knowledge in the seventeenth century.

John Evelyn

Anatomical table showing the nervous system

Anatomical table showing the placenta

THE COLLEGE AS SOLOMON'S HOUSE

The enthusiasm of the 1645 Group soon infected the rest of the College. Fellows embarked on a series of informal research projects, many of which were conducted in the College's premises at Amen Corner. The success of these activities showed the College the pragmatic benefits of remaking itself as an intellectual organisation. Not only did this allow the College to wrest back a degree of control over the shape of the new philosophy from Puritan critics, but it reinforced its position as a highly learned organisation, one increasingly pushing back the frontiers of medical knowledge.

The College outwardly signalled its change in intellectual position in several ways. It embarked on a number of communal projects of its own, setting up committees to revise the *Pharmacopoeia* and to investigate rickets. A proposal was put forward to have a laboratory built in the College. Although this was defeated, an offer from William Harvey to endow 'a library and repository for simples and rarities'[28] was accepted with alacrity. It was explicitly ordered that the new library should contain not only medical books, but should cover general books relating to the sciences. It is notable that while tomes on almost every other subject, from astronomy to zoology, were purchased, there were none on chemistry, underlying the College's ongoing dispute with the Paracelsian 'chemical' physicians. Harvey pushed the College further along the experimental path in 1656, when he donated funds for annual lectures on 'the secrets of Nature [searched out] by way of Experiment'.[29]

The College embarked on institutional reform as well. In 1647, less stringent criteria for membership of the College were introduced, a reversal of over a hundred years of College policy. New statutes were passed at the same time, governing the behaviour of members and other practitioners. There was a brief flare in regulatory activity, although the College concentrated on dangerous practitioners, rather than those practising without licences.

So successful was this programme of intellectual reform that allies of the College soon claimed it as a 'Solomon's House in reality',[30] the house having been Bacon's ideal place for the collaborative and disinterested pursuit of experimental natural philosophy.

In 1647, less stringent criteria for membership of the College were introduced, a reversal of over a hundred years of College policy.

AN ASIDE ABOUT PLAYING THE POLITICAL GAME

The question of the precise political affiliations of the College and its fellows remains unanswered. The prevailing view is that the College was predominantly Royalist in its sympathies, but displayed a degree of deftness in accommodating shifts in political power. The counterargument that the College had grown tired of the meddling of the Court in its affairs and became a genuinely revolutionary body at the outbreak of the Civil War has gained little traction.

It is intriguing, however, that several figures touted as key members of the Royalist faction of the College displayed surprising degrees of sympathy to the Parliamentarian cause. Baldwin Hamey the younger, for example, is usually held as a leader of the 'old faction' of the College. Yet Hamey was a member of the Calvinist Dutch Reformed Church of London. He was also frequently seen at sectarian rallies, a behaviour later excused by his nephew on the grounds that Hamey was secretly entertaining himself with a volume of Aristophanes bound to resemble the Greek New Testament. Similarly, George Ent, later knighted by Charles II, was an active member of the Flemish mercantile and religious community, known for its enthusiasm for Parliament. George Bate openly styled himself as a Puritan at Oxford and later became physician to Oliver Cromwell. It was only after Charles II's accession that Bate boasted of having deliberately speeded Cromwell's death.

It is difficult to judge from this distance whether the fleeting sympathies of these men for the Parliamentary cause were genuine, or born out of an instinct for survival. In any case, the aggression with which all three later distanced themselves from the 'Good Old Cause' speaks of more than just an intolerance of youthful indiscretion later regretted. It suggests an urge to erase the past completely and rewrite a different history in light of later events. Hamey's lavish bequests to the College in his older age have been interpreted as an outward sign of his deep and abiding love for it. Love, yes. But perhaps also a need for atonement for his failure to be always ideologically loyal.

It is intriguing, however, that several figures touted as key members of the Royalist faction of the College displayed surprising degrees of sympathy to the Parliamentarian cause.

...nun iudicastr, qui ad Medicinæ praxin iuxta nor-
mam Statutorum ad hoc editorum: et ad debita
privilegia, secundum rei memoriam in Annalibus
nostris servatam, admittatur. In cuius testimonium, his literis nomina nostra subscripsimus,
eademque communi sigillo munivimus. 3 Decemb:
1653.

COMITIA MENSTRUA
9 Decemb: 1653

Habita sunt a Dno Præside, quatuor Cen-
-soribus et Registario. —

Brock Dor Brock tertium examinatus probatur

Rogers Dor Georgius Rogers, Patavij: et Dor Gualterus
Myles Myles promotus Eidæ: uterque Oxoniensi elig-
-natione aucti, examen primum pro Candidatis
subierunt.

Bets Johannes Bets Artium Baccalaureus, pro Li-
-centiato, examinatur, intra Libertates.

COMITIA TRIMESTRIA
22 Decemb: 1653.

Hac sua præsentia cohonestarunt Dnus Dor
Cruisean Crosse, et Dres Wright, Alston, Hamey,
Glisson, Bathurst, Ent, Bate, Micklethwait,
Paget, Goddard, Emilie, Trench, Stanley, Benet,
Scarburgh, Wharton, Merret, Rugeley.

Brock Dres Brock et Burwell proponuntur a Præside
Burwell eligendi in numerum Permissorum in ordine ad Can-
-didatos. — Prior, omnium præterquam unius suf-
-fragijs eligitur: alteri decrant tria. —

Merret Dor Merret veniam impetrat, quoad necessaria,
reficiendi partem ædium sibi locatam, e publico
ærario. Mox etiam, proponente Dno Præside,
Collegis inter se convenit, de reparanda, et or-

-nanda tota domo Collegij.

Dni Merret, 24 Januarij 1653, demandabatur munus Anatomicum Gulstonij, in annum proximè sequentem. *[margin: Merret]*

Gregorius Walker, è Collegio Jesu, Cantabrigiensis, pro Licentiato extra libertates, examinabatur per Dnm Prujean Praesidem, et tres porro Dros Electos, Delaune, Alston, Williams Eq: Au. Feb: 9. 1653; eiçq datum est Testimonium, illi omninò geminum, quod in proxima pagina est, Timothei Woodroffe. *[margin: Gregorius Walker]*

Die secundò Februarij 1653 (qui sine pia-culo Fastis nostris eximi nequit) convenimus omnes, invitatu Dris Prujean Praesidis, et Dris Smith Electoris: nobisq averta fuit balua in novum Harvei Musaeum. ubi munificentissi-mus Senex, praesentiâ suâ, graviq ac gratâ oratione testatus benevolentiam, et omnia fausta precatus non dubitavit sese, unò mo-mento, exuere, nobisq illud integrum, condignaq supellectili ornatum dare ac dicare, quod vix aliquot annis, in summa impensarum prompti-tudine, et quotidiana operarum copia, ad culmen perductum est. Meritissimè ergo, postquam dixisset, assurrexit ei clarissimus noster Praeses, et verbis quaesitissimis, cum honorifica mentione Drii Hameij, gratias eidem, omnium Collegarum nomine, rettulit habuit. Quem statim excepit, cui id muneris, a Praeside datum, Dr Ent: qui, quâ facultate pollet, commodissimè, quae cogitet, exprimendi; rem ita totam verbis assecutus est, ut illo audito, *[margin: Inauguratio Harvaeanae Bibliothecae]*

THE COLLEGE AND OLIVER CROMWELL

The execution of Charles I in 1649 heralded a new period of political instability for the College. Over the next three years, the control of the College would swing between the Royalists and the Parliamentarians. While there is evidence of deep factional splits, such as the expulsion of several highly radicalised fellows in 1649, these changes in leadership appear to have been tactical and aimed at the College's ongoing survival. The political ferment meant that the intellectual programme became ever more important, as it gave men of opposing persuasions the opportunity to participate in activities that were deliberately constructed to be, at least on the surface, politically neutral.

Oliver Cromwell was established as Lord Protector of the Commonwealth of England, Scotland and Ireland in 1653. Unsurprisingly, the College quickly ousted the Royalist Francis Prujean and installed the Cromwellian Edward Alston, hurrying to curry favour with the new regime. The College regained some of the confidence lost during the Civil War and began to consider again how it should proceed against the irregular practitioners, who had flourished during the uncertain times. Not content with resuming regulatory activity, it sought to assert its new-found authority and make examples of those who refused to comply.

The College, however, overreached itself with the case of William Trigge, a notorious empiric. Trigge had been a thorn in the College's side since 1631, with the College and Trigge being embroiled in no fewer than six sets of legal battles, with petitions and suits eventually reaching the House of Lords. Armed with a new charter in 1656, the College set out to force Trigge to submit to their discipline. Trigge countered that the College operated an unfair monopoly and claimed the moral high ground by claiming to treat the poorer patients ignored by the physicians. Chief Justice St John threw the case out on a technicality, but then dealt the College a heavy blow, declaring that the original act of Parliament that gave the College its corporate powers had not been signed by the King. The College's original charter was therefore null and void, as were all of their subsequent charters, including the one just obtained from Cromwell, as they were based on the original act of 1523.

The College marshalled its forces. The Harveian Librarian, Christopher Merrett, delved into the archives and produced the original charter, complete with Henry VIII's signature. A new charter was obtained from Cromwell and the College began to plan how best to proceed against the empirics. But events were to overtake the College again. In 1658, Cromwell died after suffering from fever and the 'stone'. The College held its collective breath and then breathed a sigh of relief with the Restoration of the Stuart monarchy in 1660.

From a most excellent Limning, done by Samuel Cooper, in the possession of the Hon.ble Sr. Thomas Frankland Kart.

ABOVE: Oliver Cromwell
OVERLEAF: Oliver Cromwell leading his cavalry into battle (Abraham Cooper, 1787–1868) (© The Cromwell Museum, Huntingdon)

THE COLLEGE AND A NEW DAWN?

The College had survived many storms since its founding. Despite the aegis of the favour of King Henry and Cardinal Wolsey, the College was met right from the first with a degree of suspicion by virtually all other medieval institutions – the guilds, the universities, the City of London and the Church. It struggled through its first decades with a handful of members and little authority, before finding security and self-confidence under the firm hand of Caius. But behind the stern façade was an organisation riven by anxiety and doubt, and the Civil War had brought the College to the very brink of extinction. Just as the Restoration brought with it the hope of the end to turmoil and the resurrection of a stable and powerful England, so the College hoped that King Charles II would not just ensure its survival, but also restore its full authority and legitimacy. The College was sure that the very worst was finally behind it.

Exemplification of the statutes, 1673

SOURCES AND FURTHER READING

In the writing of this book, I have relied on a number of key sources (details given below). The main narrative relies heavily on Sir George Clark's two volumes of *A History of the Royal College of Physicians of London*. This has been supplemented and sometimes supplanted by the excellent work done by a small number of historians since then. The early history of the College draws on the Maddison, Pelling and Webster (eds) volume on Thomas Linacre, as well as the papers generated by the University of Padua's conference 'English Students of Medicine at the University of Padua during the Renaissance'. Pelling's work on the medieval period has heavily informed the period through to 1640, particularly her *Medical Conflicts in Early Modern London*. The way through the early scientific revolution and the Civil War was guided by Webster's magisterial *The Great Instauration*, and the subsequent fall-out by the work of Harold Cook, particularly *The Decline of the Old Medical Regime in Stuart London*. Aspects of the 'long' history of the College were informed by background work done for my presentation at the 'English Students at Padua' conference.

I have also relied on a number of other historians to provide the necessary intellectual background and additional colour. Of substantial importance are: Faye Getz on the medieval period; Jonathan Woolfson on the University of Padua; Andrew Cunningham on anatomical studies; Patrick Wallis on physicians and 'work'; Ian MacLean on the complexities of 'Galenic' medicine; Walter Ruegg's edited volumes on the University in Europe; Vivian Nutton on the life and works of John Caius; and Hugh Trevor-Roper on the life of Theodore de Mayerne.

The excellent pamphlets and historical website pages written by the archives team at the Royal College of Physicians have been liberally used, as has the illustrated history of *The Royal College of Physicians and its Collections*. Additional biographical material was obtained from the online versions of Munk's Roll [http://munksroll.rcplondon.ac.uk] and the Dictionary of National Biography [http://www.oxforddnb.com].

Axtell J.L. Education and Status in Stuart England: the London Physician. *History of Education Quarterly* 1970; 10: 141–59

Birken W.J. The Royal College of Physicians of London and Its Support of the Parliamentary Cause in the English Civil War. *Journal of British Studies* 1983; 23: 47–62

Bylebyl J. (ed). *William Harvey and His Age: The Professional and Social Context of the Discovery of Circulation*. Baltimore, Johns Hopkins University Press, 1979

Clark G. *A History of the Royal College of Physicians of London, volume 1*. Oxford, Clarendon Press, 1964

Clark G. *A History of the Royal College of Physicians of London, volume 2.* Oxford, Clarendon Press, 1966

Conrad L.I., Neve M., Nutton V., Porter R., Wear A. *The Western Medical Tradition: 800 BC to AD 1800.* Cambridge, Cambridge University Press, 1995

Cook H.J. *The Decline of the Old Medical Regime in Stuart London.* Ithaca, Cornell University Press, 1986

Cook H.J. 'Institutional Structures and Personal Belief in the London College of Physicians'. In Cunningham A., Grell O.P. (eds). *Religio Medici: Medicine and Religion in Seventeenth-Century England.* Aldershot, Scolar Press, 1996, pp. 91–114

Cunningham A. *The Anatomist Anatomis'd: An Experimental Discipline in Enlightenment Europe.* Farnham, Ashgate, 2009

Cunningham A. *The Anatomical Renaissance: The Resurrection of the Anatomical Projects of the Ancients.* Aldershot, Scolar Press, 1997

Davenport G., McDonald I., Moss-Gibbons C. (eds). *The Royal College of Physicians and its Collections: an Illustrated History.* London, James & James, 2001

Dawbarn F. 'Patronage and Power: The College of Physicians and the Jacobean Court', *British Journal for the History of Science* 1998; 31: 1–19

de Ridder-Symoens H. (ed). *A History of the University in Europe: volume I, Universities in the Middle Ages.* Cambridge, Cambridge University Press, 1992

de Ridder-Symoens H. (ed). *A History of the University in Europe: volume II, Universities in Early Modern Europe (1500–1800).* Cambridge, Cambridge University Press, 1996

Field J.V., James F.A.J.L. (eds). *Renaissance and Revolution: Humanists, Scholars, Craftsmen and Natural Philosophers in Early Modern Europe.* Cambridge, Cambridge University Press, 1994

Furdell E. *The Royal Doctors, 1485–1714: Medical Personnel at the Tudor and Stuart Courts.* Rochester, University of Rochester Press, 2001

Gadd I.A., Wallis P. (eds). *Guilds, Society and Economy in London 1450–1800.* London, Centre for Metropolitan History, 2002

Getz F. *Medicine in the English Middle Ages.* Princeton, Princeton University Press, 1998

Grell O.P., Cunningham A., Arrizabalaga J. (eds). *Centres of Medical Excellence? Medical Travel and Education in Europe, 1500–1789*. Farnham, Ashgate, 2009

Jenner M.S.R., Wallis P. (eds). *Medicine and the Market in England and its Colonies, c.1450–c.1850*. Basingstoke, Palgrave Macmillan, 2007

Maclean I. *Logic, Signs and Nature in the Renaissance: The Case of Learned Medicine*. Cambridge, Cambridge University Press, 2002

Maddison F., Pelling M., Webster C. (eds). *Essays on the Life and Work of Thomas Linacre, c.1460–1524*. Oxford, Clarendon Press, 1977

Marrone D., Luxon L., Thiene G. (eds). *English Students of Medicine at the University of Padua During the Renaissance*. Padua, Padova University Press, 2016 [in press]

Nutton V. *John Caius and the Manuscripts of Galen*. Cambridge, Cambridge Philological Society, 1987

Nutton V. 'Greek Science in the sixteenth-century Renaissance'. In Field J.V., James F.A.J.L. (eds), *Renaissance and Revolution: Humanists, Scholars, Craftsmen and Natural Philosophers in Early Modern Europe*. Cambridge, Cambridge University Press, 1994, pp. 15–28

Pelling M. *The Common Lot: Sickness, Medical Occupations and the Urban Poor in Early Modern England*. London, Longman, 1998

Pelling M. *Medical Conflicts in Early Modern London: Patronage, Physicians, and Irregular Practitioners 1550–1640*. Oxford, Clarendon Press, 2003

Sharp L. 'The Royal College of Physicians and Interregnum Politics'. *Medical History* 1975; 19: 107–28

Trevor-Roper H. *Europe's Physician: The Various Life of Sir Theodore de Mayerne*. New Haven and London, Yale University Press, 2006

Webster C. *The Great Instauration: Science, Medicine and Reform 1626–1660*, 2nd edn. Oxford, Peter Lang, 2002

Woolfson J. *Padua and the Tudors: English Students in Italy, 1485–1603*. Cambridge, James Clarke & Co, 1998

ENDNOTES

1. John Freind. *The History of Physick: from the Time of Galen, to the Beginning of the Sixteenth Century*. Chiefly with regard to Practice, in a Discourse written to Doctor Mead. London, J. Walthoe, 1725.

2. Aldine Manutius. Cited in F. Maddison, M. Pelling, C. Webster (eds). *Essays on the Life and Work of Thomas Linacre, c.1460–1524*. Oxford, Clarendon Press, 1977, p. xix.

3. George Lily, cited in Maddison, ibid, p. xvii.

4. Freind, op. cit.

5. Margaret Pelling. *Medical Conflicts in Early Modern London: Patronage, Physicians, and Irregular Practitioners 1550–1640*. Oxford, Clarendon Press, 2003, p. 231.

6. Hippocrates, cited in G.E.R. Lloyd (ed), *Hippocratic Writings*. Harmondsworth, Penguin, 1983, p. 262.

7. Charles Webster. *The Great Instauration: Science, Medicine and Reform 1626–1660*, 2nd edn. Oxford, Peter Lang, 2002, p. 201.

8. Faye Getz. *Medicine in the English Middle Ages*. Princeton, Princeton University Press, 1998, p. 70.

9. An Act Confirming the Jurisdiction of the Bishops, 3 Henry VIII, c.11, 1512. Cited in Clark, op. cit., p. 54.

10. The Founding Charter of 1518. MS4917, Archives of the Royal College of Physicians. Translation kindly provided by the College.

11. Oxford Dictionaries, Oxford University Press, 2016, http://www.oxforddictionaries.com/definition/english/socius (accessed 26 April 2016).

12. Indenture Between the Warden of Merton College and Edmond Cryspyne. Cited in Maddison, op. cit., p. 211,

13. An Act Confirming the Charter, 14 & 15 Henry VIII, c.5, 1523. Archives of the Royal College of Physicians. Translation kindly provided by the College.

14. Clark, op. cit., vol. 1, p. 92.

15. Clark, ibid., vol. 1, p. 80.

16 Will of Thomas Linacre. Cited in Maddison, op. cit., p. 166.

17. Andrew Wear. *Knowledge and Practice in English Medicine, 1550–1680*. Cambridge, Cambridge University Press, 2000, p. 132.

18. Christopher Merrett. Cited in J.L. Axtell. 'Education and Status in Stuart England: the London Physician', *History of Education Quarterly* 1970, vol. 10, pp. 141–59, p. 148.

19. Clark, op. cit., vol. 1 p. 136.

20. Elizabeth Furdell. *The Royal Doctors, 1485–1714: Medical Personnel at the Tudor and Stuart Courts*, Rochester, University of Rochester Press, 2001, p. 84.

21. Disorders in the College of Phistions. Cited in Clark, op. cit., p. 129.

22. Clark, ibid., vol. 1, p. 222.

23. Clark, ibid., vol. 1, p. 159.

24. Certaine Statutes, sigs. K3–N4. Cited in Harold J. Cook. 'Policing the Health of London: The College of Physicians and the Early Stuart Monarch', *Social History of Medicine* 1989, vol. 2, p. 1–33.

25. Annals of the Royal College of Physicians. Cited in Harold J. Cook. *The Decline of the Old Medical Regime in Stuart London*. Ithaca, Cornell University Press, 1986, p. 99.

26. Thomas Rand. Cited in Webster, op cit., p. 307.

27. William Harvey, cited in Andrew Cunningham 'William Harvey' in P. Harriman and S. Mitton (eds). *Cambridge Scientific Minds*. Cambridge, Cambridge University Press, 2002, p. 30.

28. Webster, op. cit., p. 320.

29. William Munk. Cited in Webster, ibid., p. 321.

30. Walter Charleton. Cited in Webster, ibid., p. 315.

Map of former RCP locations showing Knightrider Street, Amen Corner and a later site in Warwick Lane